SHAFTESBURY

The Poor Man's Earl

SHAFTESBURY

The Poor Man's Earl

John Pollock

HODDER AND STOUGHTON
LONDON SYDNEY AUCKLAND TORONTO

For
Timothy Dudley-Smith

British Library Cataloguing in Publication Data

Pollock, John, *1923–*
  Shaftesbury: the poor man's earl.
  1. Shaftesbury, Anthony Ashley Cooper, *Earl of,*
  1801–1885
  I. Title
  941.081'092'4   DA565.S4/

  ISBN 0-340-37281-8 Pbk
  ISBN 0-340-38275-9 Hbk

CONTENTS

8   CONTENTS

FOREWORD

'Our Earl's gone! God A'mighty knows he loved us, and we loved him. We shan't see his likes again!'

These words of a 'poor labouring man in tattered garments, but with a piece of crêpe sewed on to his sleeve', as he watched a flower-laden coffin carried out of Westminster Abbey one autumn day in 1885, have rung down the years. The vast crowd in Parliament Square bowed and still, the Costermongers' Temperance Society's Band playing 'Safe in the Arms of Jesus', and the great congregation in the Abbey, from peers and bishops to flower-girls and crippled boys, quietly leaving their places after the service – the funeral of Lord Shaftesbury is one of the famous scenes of the later nineteenth century.

Shaftesbury's work for the poor will never be forgotten. His place in history is secure. In the very different world of a century later, when most of the social reforms for which he fought are taken for granted, the principles by which he lived remain vital. It is important to know what he was, not merely what he did; how his character was shaped and moulded; the light and tone of his personality from youth to old age.

This short book aims to tell Shaftesbury's story in such a way that he comes alive as his contemporaries knew him. It is based partly on new material which has come to light at his home, St. Giles's House near Wimborne in Dorset, and I am most grateful to the Earl of Shaftesbury for drawing my attention to these papers and letting me use them. I also wish to thank his Archivist, Mrs. Elspeth Griffiths, B.A., whose patient help meant a great deal to this book, and his private secretary, Mrs. C. Lowe. I am also grateful to the Trustees of the Broadlands Archives Trust and especially to Lord Brabourne for allowing me to consult and quote from the Seventh Earl's diaries and other papers which were in the possession of his son Evelyn Ashley, and the papers of Lord Mount-Temple.

A book of this size must be based mainly on printed sources. Edwin Hodder's great official *Life and Work of the Seventh Earl of Shaftesbury, K.G.* (three volumes, 1886) is still important. I have also used contemporary magazines and books, and I am specially grateful to Mr. Robert Heasman, public relations officer of the Shaftesbury Society, who brought down a pile of rare books to my home in Devon on loan.

I owe a big debt of thanks to Mrs. Georgina Battiscombe, author of *Shaftesbury: A Biography of the Seventh Earl,* published by Constable in 1974, and to Professor Geoffrey B. A. M. Finlayson, author of *The Seventh Earl of Shaftesbury 1801–1885,* published by Methuen London in 1981. These authors and their publishers have allowed me to quote material first published in their books. I am particularly grateful to Mrs. Battiscombe who most generously lent me her research notes: I have in fact used several manuscripts which she discovered but did not quote in her own book. Readers who wish to follow Shaftesbury's campaigns blow by blow, to analyse his character in depth or study his political opinions and actions in detail should refer to these distinguished books, both based on a wide range of original sources, though my own interpretation differs in some respects from each.

I gratefully acknowledge the gracious permission of Her Majesty The Queen to make use of material in the Royal Archives and of material not in the Royal Archives but of which the copyright belongs to Her Majesty.

I also thank the following: The Earl of Harrowby, for permission to see and quote from letters written by Shaftesbury to the third earl when Lord Sandon, and his archivist, Mrs. Jane Waley; Sir Hereward Wake, Bt., for permission to quote from unpublished writing of Charlotte

Lady Wake; Miss Maclean of Ardgour, for lending me Shaftesbury's letters to the Burns family; Mr. Alexander Chinnery-Haldane of Gleneagles; the Church Pastoral Aid Society (Mission at Home) and its general secretary, the Rev. David R. Bubbers; the Falcon Press for permission to use some material, and the title, from a booklet I wrote about Shaftesbury some years ago; the London City Mission and its editorial secretary, Mr. Stanley Seymour; the Rt. Rev. Timothy Dudley-Smith, Bishop of Thetford; Miss Shirley Ansell; Dr. Raymond Brown of Spurgeon's College; Mr. David Holland, C.B.E.; the Rev. J. S. Reynolds; the archivists of Harrow School and of Christ Church, Oxford; the Chief Archivist of Northamptonshire County Record Office, Mr P. I. King; the Central Librarian, Chesterfield; the Department of Paleography and Diplomatic, University of Durham; the staffs of the National Register of Archives, the Hampshire Record Office and the Oxfordshire Record Office; the London Library; the Salford Museum of Mining, and the Science Museum.

Finally I would like to thank Mrs. J. E. Williams of Bideford, north Devon, who once again has typed my manuscript with such skill; and my publisher, David Wavre of Hodder and Stoughton.

John Pollock,
Rose Ash, Devonshire

PROLOGUE

The man at the pithead wheel was astonished that an aristocrat should step into the open bucket to descend. He would come up filthy with coal dust, his face black as the bodies of the little boys and girls who, every day until a few months back, had clung to each other in this bucket, weary after hours of labour underground. But the manager said that this was Lord Ashley, M.P., the man who had made Parliament free the children and women from the mines.

The engineman stoked his boiler and started the winch. As Lord Ashley knew, the shaft of this pit in south Lancashire was 450 feet deep, a greater drop than the height of Salisbury Cathedral spire, the highest in the land, with nothing between him and death but the cable on the bucket and the attentiveness of the engineman: at least Ashley would not be in the hands of a child, this September of 1842: as he had told the House of Commons in June, children cost lives. In one accident several persons were killed because the child at the engine had chased a mouse instead of applying the brake.

Ashley, with a wife and family, had no desire to be killed in a coal mine but, as he recorded laconically: 'Thought it a duty: easier to talk after you have seen. So away I went, and had ever in my mind, "Underneath are the everlasting arms" – so I feared not.'

At the bottom with the smell of coal and damp in the ill-ventilated air, and the guttering candlelight, Ashley could imagine the terror of small children starting work at the age of six or younger. His Act of Parliament would not come into force for another six months but this mine had

been inherited by two of his dearest friends and they had
abolished the labour of children and women underground,
even before his Bill had become law.

The children were gone, but Ashley's heart went out to
the donkeys who pulled the trucks and never saw the light
of day. Many had weals from cruel drivers.

The manager took candles and led him towards the
seams. Ashley climbed ladders, knowing that boys and
girls had clambered down with baskets of coals on their
backs, secured by straps round their heads. He stooped
along galleries, where children on all fours had dragged
and pushed the heavy sleds of coal. Some mines had seams
so low that they could be worked only by a naked small boy,
lying on his back hacking with a little pick. These boys
nearly all grew up deformed. His Act would close such
seams.

He reached a coal face. In the dim light he saw the
colliers, stark naked except for footwear. He watched them
wield their picks. Until August children and youths of both
sexes, nearly naked themselves, had worked beside them
shovelling the coal into the sleds; hour after hour in the heat
and bad air they had been kept at hard labour, often
punished or abused by the men.

Child labour throughout the mines would end soon. The
Commons had listened to Ashley. The House of Lords had
tried to avoid considering his Bill but it had passed at
last, with Ashley 'in joyful and humble thankfulness to
Almighty God'.

He had saved these children, but other crusades were
far from victory.

When he went down the mine Ashley was on a week's
visit to the Manchester neighbourhood. He had met cotton
masters and tried to persuade them that they would not be
ruined if children were prevented by law from working
more than ten hours a day in the mills. He had been
presented with an Address by his allies in this long campaign for Ten Hours, and had delivered a rousing reply:
'Over a large surface of the industrial community, man has
been regarded as an animal . . . Women and children

follow in the train of ceaseless toil and degrading occupation, and thus we have before us a mighty multitude of
feeble bodies and untaught minds . . .'

On the Saturday night he had seen what this could mean
to a community. Guided by two police inspectors, he had
walked through the slums of Manchester as he already
walked the slums of London. He saw afresh the need for
better housing and health, and for care of souls as well as
bodies. The chief constable had told him that the borough
of Manchester (not yet a city) in that year of 1842 had 1267
public houses or beer houses, 695 brothels of one sort or
another, and 763 street walkers. Ashley 'passed through
cellars, garrets, gin-palaces, beer houses, brothels, gaming
houses, and every sort of vice and violence.'

Suddenly, 'in the very depth of dirt and uproar,' he saw
'a darling little girl seven years old . . . Never did I witness
such beauty of natural, untaught affection towards its
rough and unkind mother. I determined, God willing, to
rescue it if possible.'

Such a scene would awaken memories of his own miserable childhood, not in a mine but a mansion; and of the one
person who had befriended him. Late that night, as the
policemen accompanied him in a cab to the house where he
was the guest of old friends, it was a natural action to take
out his gold watch. Then he would say: 'This watch belonged to the best friend I ever had in the world.'

Thirty-one years had passed since she died . . .

Part One

Young Lord Ashley
1801–1851

1

THE GOLD WATCH

Master Anthony was cold, hungry and miserable. His father was heir to an earldom and his mother was the daughter of a duke, but they were badly off and devoted to the high life of fashion. They seem to have looked on Anthony and his three elder sisters (and the five sons that followed him) as little more than the consequences of love-life and the need to carry on the line.

Anthony Ashley Cooper had been born on 28 April 1801 in the London house of his uncle, the fifth Earl of Shaftesbury, who lived abroad with his wife and daughter. Anthony's father, the Honourable Cropley Ashley, M.P., generally dropped the family name of Cooper, and thus could answer to 'Ashley', which would have been his courtesy title had he been heir to a father instead of a brother; even his mother addressed him as Ashley. He married Lady Anne Spencer, daughter of the fourth Duke of Marlborough. Her mother, herself the daughter of a duke, was disliked by Queen Charlotte as 'the proudest woman in England'.

The Ashleys went about their concerns and amusements. The household budget was tight. The servants cared little if they ate most of the food before the time for nursery supper; or if the coal scuttles had not been refilled on a cold night. When the parents were at home the children were more miserable still, for Cropley Ashley bullied them by tongue and hand.

The six-year-old Anthony, however, had one friend, a

housekeeper who seemed very old to him though she was only in her forties. Anna Maria Milles (pronounced Millis – hence the misspelling which went into the history books) had been a servant at Blenheim Palace. In 1785, at the age of twenty-five, she had been appointed personal maid to Lady Anne, then about twelve years old. Known thenceforth as Maria, she remained Lady Anne's 'confidential servant and friend', moving into the Ashley household after the wedding in 1796. By 1807 she seems to have been retired as lady's maid: she may have had weak health. She held the rank of housekeeper, without domestic authority but with a room of her own, and Anthony was entrusted to her care. He probably learned his letters with her, and grew devoted to Maria Milles, the only grown-up to show him affection.

Each evening, before a nursemaid came to hurry him off for bed, Maria would take him on her knee and tell him stories from the Gospels and teach him how to pray. She told him of Calvary and the Empty Tomb and spoke of the Lord Jesus as the risen Redeemer who could be a Friend. A strong simple faith like hers, which Whitefield and Wesley had preached afresh to thousands in the open fields, and in parlours, was rare in aristocratic households, above or below stairs. Since Blenheim's parish of Woodstock with Bladon was not Evangelical, and since she was not baptised at either church, the intriguing possibility is that Maria Milles came from a little village nearby where one of John Wesley's early supporters, George Stonhouse, once vicar of Islington but later a Moravian, was living in retirement.

Anthony understood what she told him, and believed. Long afterwards, a few years before his death, he was walking in the park of his country mansion in Dorset with some of those who helped him in his work for the London poor, 'when the topic of conversation turned upon conversion – change of heart – the new birth. It soon became manifest that the subject was not only thoroughly understood, but had been personally experienced.' The aged earl told them, as he had told many others, about Maria Milles and how she had led him 'to "seek first the Kingdom of God," and rest not until he had found it'. As he remembered her his voice faltered 'and his eyes filled, and before touching on another subject he added, "God be praised for her, and for her loving faithfulness; we shall meet by-and-by in the House where there are many mansions."'

Anthony was sent at the age of seven to a large fashionable boarding school at Chiswick, conveniently placed between the Ashleys' London house and their country home at Richmond on the river. It had once been a good school but Dr. Horne was growing old and depended on the rod. The place was dirty, the food poor, and the bigger boys bullied the younger. Anthony was a highly sensitive child and hated the pain; he made no real friends and expected every hand to be against him. The place, he considered in retrospect, had no compensating advantage 'except, perhaps, it may have given me an early horror of oppression and cruelty.'

In the holidays he had his brothers and sisters to play with and the friendship of Maria Milles, but on 9 June 1811, when he was ten, and away at school, Maria died in her fifty-first year; Anthony never heard where she was buried. He mourned grievously and felt alone in the world. Despite the jeers of other boys he took refuge in the Bible she had taught him to love, and prayed to the Friend they shared; one prayer in particular, which he had learned from Maria, he used every day for the rest of his life but never committed to paper.

Maria ('*most* truly your affectionate friend') left him her gold watch, which perhaps was an heirloom presented to her father after long years of service on the Blenheim estate. Anthony wore it always and in after years would often show it, saying, 'This belonged to the best friend I ever had.'[1]

*   *   *

1. Details concerning Anna Maria Milles emerged when the present Lord Shaftesbury discovered in 1984 a little octagonal locket, decorated with a bird in a tree (possibly a partridge in a pear tree) which Maria may have worn. It is inscribed on the side: *Anna Maria Milles. Born Oct. 23rd 1760. Died June 9th 1811.* On the bottom is: *Twenty Six years the confidential servant and friend of Anne Countess of Shaftesbury.* The gold watch has not been traced.

That summer of 1811 Anthony's uncle the earl died at the age of forty-nine, of wrongly diagnosed dropsy: 'My poor brother,' noted Cropley, 'fell a victim to Dr. Pere Eliza's ignorance and conceit.' Cropley succeeded as sixth Earl of Shaftesbury and Anthony was known thenceforth by the courtesy title of Lord Ashley. In the manner of the times his Christian name disappeared: he was Ashley to his relations and intimates and Lord Ashley to the world. The family did not become much better off, for the late earl's daughter ('as stupid as a post') was left a large part of the fortune, while the new earl had all the expense of the encumbered family estates in Dorset and Hampshire. This sixth Earl of Shaftesbury, a thorough Tory, spent most of the next forty years as the efficient, brusque, unpopular chairman of committees (Deputy Speaker) in the House of Lords.

In the autumn of 1813 Ashley was drearily parsing Latin or Greek at Manor House when his father the earl drove up and took him away, and straight to Harrow School, though he himself had been at Winchester. Handing him over the earl remarked that he knocked the boy down and recommended the tutor to do the same.

Harrow had been ruled since 1805 by young Dr. George Butler, ancestor of notable academics and public servants, including R. A. Butler. The headmaster was athletic, versatile and accomplished. Ashley was placed in his house as a boarder and soon began to burgeon. He grew tall. He loved physical exercise, especially boxing, though despite a quick temper he never had a stand-up fight. These were always bare fisted like prize-fights, therefore technically illegal, yet common enough at public schools: ten years later one of Ashley's young brothers died after a plucky two hour fight with a bigger boy at Eton, while most of the school watched. He was plied with brandy between rounds, refused to give up, and when he fell unconscious his own brother John thought he would revive without medical aid, until too late.

In retrospect Ashley thought himself idle at Harrow and too fond of amusements; but he won prizes and reached the under sixth form, which sat with the sixth, before his

fifteenth birthday. He made friends. Away from his intimi-
dating father and unfeeling mother he showed a great
sense of humour. Yet the early years of unhappiness had
left their mark. If he were alone, 'a fine summer's evening
had the effect of melancholy over my heart.'

Suddenly, in the year after Waterloo, before he was
sixteen, Ashley was confronted by an incident which
changed his life.

He was walking alone down Harrow Hill when he heard
shouting and yelling, and then drunken singing. He
stopped. To his disgust he saw four or five tipsy men
lurching up a side street under the weight of a rough coffin,
the kind used only for paupers. As they turned the corner
on their way to the churchyard one of them stumbled and
the coffin fell to the ground. The men let out a stream of
oaths.

Ashley felt sick. A fellow human being was to be buried,
with no mourner, his remains degraded by the drunken
antics of men who cared nothing. 'Good heavens!' thought
Ashley. 'Can this be permitted simply because the man was
poor and friendless?'

In the perspective of the years he saw this event as: 'the
origin of my public career . . . It brought powerfully before
me the scorn and neglect manifested towards the poor and
helpless. I was deeply affected, but for many years afterwards I acted only on feeling and sentiment. As I advanced
in life, all this grew up to a sense of duty; and I was
convinced that God had called me to devote whatever
advantages He might have bestowed upon me in the cause
of the weak, the helpless, both man and beast, and those
who had none to help them.'

2

AN ANGEL IN VIENNA

Against the magnificent backdrop of Castle Howard, one August day of 1820, the nineteen-year-old Lord Ashley was tumbling down the grass slopes with eight-year-old Blanche Howard, one of the numerous sisters of his great friend George Howard, grandson of the Earl of Carlisle. Then they played billiards, for though Ashley liked the company of her elder sister Harriet, and enjoyed sport with George, he always had time for small children, who adored him.

Ashley was now very good looking. Though not quite six foot he was above the average height of the day. Slender but strongly built and holding himself almost too erect, he had a mass of jet-black curly hair, contrasting with a particularly white skin, which was untouched by sunburn because gentlemen always wore hats out of doors. Even before he reached maturity Ashley's features were pronounced – an aquiline nose, a firm, rather prominent chin and a full mouth. His light blue eyes were deep-set, under unusually prominent eyelids which gave a hooded effect. The ladies were inclined to fall in love with him.

His father had taken him away from Harrow, to his sorrow, in December 1816 when he was still fifteen and already the twentieth senior boy in a school of nearly three hundred: possibly the earl wanted to save the cost of the fees. Ashley was sent in term-times during the next two years to a first cousin and her husband, the Reverend Frederick Ricketts, rector of Eckington near Chesterfield in north Derbyshire. The Ricketts were straight out of Jane Austen: the rector was young, elegant and very well connected; his wife, as the niece of an earl, was always dressed in the height of fashion. They had one infant.

Ricketts was not expected to teach anything. Ashley was intended for the Army, which required no brains, and he hardly opened a book, but roamed around with his gun and the dogs; if he took an interest in the coal-miners and iron-workers of the parish he never recalled it. He became great friends with young Sir George Sitwell, the lord of the manor who lived at Renishaw nearby, and his bride, Susan Tait, eldest sister of the future archbishop. The Sitwells (ancestors of the writers Osbert and Edith) were a happy, hospitable pair who helped Ashley enjoy a time of freedom to offset the miseries of his childhood. Lady Sitwell described Ashley to her sister Charlotte in Edinburgh as a magnificently handsome youth, 'full of fun and frolic'; when he came up to their parties he was 'the most frolicsome of them all'.

Holidays were overshadowed by dread of his father but they were partly spent exploring the family estate at Wimborne St. Giles in Dorset, which Ashley's ancestors had held since the Norman Conquest, and the neighbouring wild country of Cranborne Chase. One day in the park at St. Giles he came on an old chalk pit. He was already interested in science and it occurred to him that lumps of chalk could be used to line the grates of poor cottagers, to refract heat and save fuel. It was not until many years later that he tried the experiment but the thought showed that the vow at Harrow was not entirely forgotten.

Ashley did not want to go into the Army, despite being a descendant of Marlborough, and was relieved when the earl changed his mind under pressure from Lord Bathurst, one of several peers, including the Iron Duke himself, who did what they could to supply the place of a father to Ashley and his brothers; in the close-knit world of society the Shaftesburys were much criticised for their treatment of the children.

Ashley therefore went up in 1819 to Christ Church,

Oxford, the college of his father and grandfather. He turned his back on idleness and read for an honours degree, which required a mastery of the Greek and Latin classics.

It was here that he made friends with George Howard, and for part of their first Long Vacation, 1820, they planned a tour of Scotland, setting off from Castle Howard. On their way home they came to Edinburgh where the Sitwells were already staying in the British Hotel so that Susan could be near her family, the Taits, for the birth of her second child.

Charlotte Tait (afterwards Lady Wake) now 'made acquaintance with Lord Ashley, of whom I had heard so much at Renishaw. I thought him the handsomest young man I had ever seen: he was very tall, and his countenance radiant with youthful brightness.' Ashley wanted to make George Howard 'as intimate with his friends as he was himself, but Mr. Howard was, besides being naturally shy, quite a stranger, and did not see the pleasure or advantage of this; and I remember being infinitely amused by the manner in which the introduction was effected. We heard a sort of laughing scuffle at the drawing-room door, which was suddenly thrown open from the outside, and he was projected head foremost into the midst of us like a battering-ram, while Lord Ashley shouted out, "Enter the Honourable George Howard." Of course after this there was an end of all shyness.'

For Christmas that year Ashley wanted Howard to stay at 'The Saint', as he always called St. Giles's House. 'Every old lute, harp and dulcimer will be put in requisition, old fowling pieces and blunderbusses to furnish a salute.' Howard came, and found that Ashley and his next younger brother, William, would not open 'either of their well-formed mouths in the presence of their sire'; but apart from 'uncommon awe and reserve' towards the earl, the whole family of brothers and sisters proved delightful, though Caroline made the tea 'abominably weak'.

George Howard's mother, known as Lady Georgiana Morpeth until her husband succeeded to the earldom of Carlisle, and her sister Lady Granville gave Ashley affection and kindness which he missed from his mother. Lady Georgiana tried to cure him of his tendency to impulsive, violent expressions of opinion. He wrote to her playfully: 'I cannot exactly decide, but I rather think that I have not been so violent and impetuous as formerly. Howard perhaps will say differently; there is little doubt however that in time I should grow cool; you will remark, like the lava, cold at the surface but heated at the bottom.'

Ashley was determined to make a great name for himself. He lay awake at nights dreaming of fame and immortality, and therefore worked hard, unlike most of the gold-tasselled noblemen of Christ Church, though he enjoyed the delights of Oxford. After three years he gained his First. To be placed in the First Class of an honours degree showed a first class brain. He had found much happiness, made lasting friendships, overcome difficulties, and now, as he went down at the age of twenty-one 'all around seems to be in the fairest prospect, and if my father behaved with common kindness I should be at present in perfect tranquillity.'

His father gave him a comparatively small allowance and left him to shift for himself, and to stay chiefly at the homes of his friends rather than at St. Giles's or Grosvenor Square: these friends tended to be Whigs, which may have displeased the rigidly Tory earl. A Tory seat in the House of Commons would be found but the next General Election was at least three years ahead. Ashley decided to extend the customary Grand Tour on the Continent to two whole years. On 27 August 1823 he and an Oxford friend set out for Calais by new-fangled steam boat from Tower Stairs in London, to the relief of Lady Holland, the celebrated Whig hostess, who said that Ashley was so 'very handsome and captivating' that 'his absence will be a blessing to young ladies.' They misinterpreted kindness as courtship and she thought him cold hearted not to respond.

His Grand Tour took him through Switzerland to Naples and Rome and finally to Vienna, with his brother William, in August 1824. Here occurred an event almost as decisive as the lessons at Maria Milles's knee and the pauper funeral at Harrow: he fell head over heels in love with an unsuitable girl.

Antoinette von Leykham was beautiful, vivacious and well read but she was the offspring of a *mésalliance*: her father, a baron and minor diplomat, had married an opera singer, so that they were not received in Vienna society. Their house was full of undesirable characters: Ashley's 'Liebe, dear Liebe', as he called her, 'was and is an angel,' he wrote the following year, 'but she was surrounded by and would have brought with her a halo of hell.'

'Man has never loved more furiously or more imprudently,' he wrote. He determined to marry her and 'I thought the Deity harsh in the obstacles to our Union.' These probably included strong dissuasion by the British Ambassador, Lord Cowley, the Duke of Wellington's brother, who would have seen it as his duty to block a marriage which might jeopardise Ashley's social and political future. Ashley himself, deep in his heart, knew the imprudence of his furious wooing, for a Roman Catholic wife, even without shady connections, would create embarrassments in those years before Roman Catholic Emancipation.

And, when he forced himself to face reality, he knew that 'Liebe' and her surroundings would not foster his faith.

He had never ceased to pray, every night, the prayer he had learned from Maria Milles; but in the nine or ten years since the incident at Harrow his Christianity seems to have flickered. The evidence is thin but suggests that by 1825 Ashley's personal faith was little more than an inward light to keep him from evil such as the fornication which was characteristic of young aristocrats in the reign of George IV; or to incline him to kindnesses such as asking a plain wallflower for a dance. He had received little help from parents or private tutor: 'I was brought up in the high and dry school,' he would say, which held the Church of England to be primarily a prop of the political structure of the realm, and regarded Dissenters and Methodists as wicked. His sisters Charlotte, Caroline and Harriet

weighted the scale the other way, for Maria Milles seems to
have touched their lives too.

At Oxford Ashley was not counted an Evangelical. In the
two and a half years since coming down he had done
nothing of value by his own estimation; he thought himself
mentally lazy and confused. He remained very ambitious.
Sometimes he dreamed of being a great and rich political
leader, exerting his influence 'for the increase of religion
and true happiness'. At other times he pursued what he
afterwards called 'false reasoning', which may have been a
study of the works of his great-grandfather, the philosopher third earl, whose *Characteristicks* was a potent
contribution to the Deism which dominated eighteenth-
century thought.

Had Ashley been wooed from Christianity by his ancestor he would have become a man of the past rather than of
the future; but his hopeless love for 'Liebe' forced him to
discover himself. He realised the strength of his sexual
passions and that he needed the controlling influence of a
power greater than himself. He could no longer limp between two opinions: he must choose between the flesh and
the Spirit; to be conformed to the world or be transformed
by the renewing of his mind.

He made the choice. He chose the path of dedication.
Whether the affair with Antoinette ended first, precipitat-
ing his decision, or whether he drew back as a result of it
cannot be known because years later he tore the relevant
pages from his diary.

Ashley and Antoinette stayed friends. He wrote occasionally and when the great Austrian statesman Prince
Metternich, a widower, astonished the world by making
her his second wife Ashley rejoiced at the brilliant match
and her happy marriage. When she died giving birth to
Metternich's heir he grieved for his 'Liebe' but did not
regret that their love had been ended: he had accepted
God's 'wisdom and tender Providence: "he doeth all for the
best."'

By early August 1825 Ashley was back in England. From
now on he sought to deepen his Christian understanding,

especially studying the Bible with Thomas Scott's Commentary. The growth of Ashley's spiritual perceptions at this period cannot yet be charted accurately, but he developed a strong sense of responsibility, accepting that his advantages of birth were given for the benefit of the less fortunate. He looked for a worthy line of life and was full of enthusiasm to make the world a better place.

Seriousness did not destroy his sense of humour. Lady Granville's eldest son, the future Foreign Secretary, then a boy at Eton, got to know Ashley about this time and noticed particularly the glee with which he retailed jokes against himself. Granville said of him after his death: 'I have hardly ever known any man with a greater sense of humour than himself, or with a greater appreciation of humour in other persons.'

Even the gouty old king enjoyed Ashley's humour. 'I have spent a most happy time,' Ashley recorded after a visit to Royal Lodge in the last year of George IV. 'Such a round of laughing and pleasure I never enjoyed; if there is a hospitable gentleman on earth it is His Majesty. I was so jovial I almost forgot myself, but now I say with Job, "It may be I have sinned and cursed God in my heart," but I trust not. I was harmless in my mirth.'

*　　　*　　　*

In 1826 Ashley entered the unreformed House of Commons, six years before the Great Reform Bill and eight before the fire: the House still sat in St. Stephen's Chapel, with trees visible through the windows behind the Speaker's chair. He and his older cousin Blandford had been elected for Woodstock, a seat controlled by his uncle the Duke of Marlborough. Ashley 'took the oaths of Parliament with great goodwill – a slight prayer for assistance in my thoughts and deeds.'

He soon found that he needed both humour and divine assistance. Unfair attacks on his Tory friends by Radical M.P.s made his blood boil. Experienced Members scarcely noticed invective, but young Lord Ashley, his good man-

ners preserving him in outward composure, was upset.
Going home he poured out his feelings into the diary which
was to prove his safety valve in the years to come: 'I am too
bilious for public life. What I suffer from the brazen faced
and low insults of the Radical party! . . . I should have
stormed in madness had it been against myself. I am not fit
for the House of Commons.'

The world disagreed. Though he had not yet made his
maiden speech he was good on committees and the House
thought highly of him as a rising star. His patron and hero
the Duke of Wellington wished to bring him forward and
had him to stay at Stratfield Saye; Ashley listened entranced as they walked or rode together, and he lapped
up those pithy comments and reminiscences now found
in books of quotations. On the other side of the House
Henry Brougham, the radical Whig lawyer, who sat with
Ashley on a Select Committee, wrote to Lady Jersey: 'I have
a high opinion of him as an uncommon young man, and in
spite of his father I hope great and good things of him.'
Brougham was loud in his praises to Lady Carlisle, as Lady
Georgiana Morpeth had become, and she passed them back
to Ashley.

Ashley was elated; then he would be thrown into
depression, convinced of his inadequacy. He puzzled
sometimes that he should pass so swiftly from elation
to depression, and contemplated retiring into private life to
become a man of letters; or, since his hobbies were
mathematics and astronomy, he might devote his days to
science. He loved languages too, and when his sister Charlotte married a landowner near the Welsh border he learned
Welsh. Visions of achieving political leadership and making England a fount of goodness and happiness for all the
world were overshadowed by a strong diffidence and a
tendency to introspection. He was also, in Lord Bathurst's
words, 'mighty sensitive', which could be fatal to a
politician.

Not surprisingly, he began to suffer stomach complaints,
which are often caused by stress. All his long life he would
be hampered by the mix of characteristics which came with

his Shaftesbury and Marlborough blood, including a touch
of Duchess Sarah's famous temper.

Ashley was well liked. Friends and political seniors respected him too as an undisguised Christian, and were
unaware that his religion might make him an awkward
colleague in government. However, when Canning formed
his administration in April 1827 Ashley declined a place,
the first rung on the ladder, out of loyalty to Wellington. 'It
is a great loss to me but I have done rightly.'

He still did not know what he would make of his life.
Then, in June 1827, he served on another Select Committee
of the House, his fourth. The subject was: 'On Pauper
Lunatics in the County of Middlesex and on Lunatic
Asylums.'

As he listened to the evidence he was appalled, and
remembered his vow on Harrow Hill.

3

THE LUNATICS OF BETHNAL GREEN

During the hot June of 1827 the small room at Westminster seemed stifling as the members of the all-Party Select Committee, including the Home Secretary, listened to pauper patients and parish overseers as they gave evidence about Thomas Warburton's madhouse, the White House at Bethnal Green.

One overseer of the poor described the place where incontinent patients were confined: 'A crib-room,' he said, 'is a place where there is nothing but wooden cribs or bedsteads, cases in fact, filled with straw and covered with a blanket, in which these unfortunate beings are placed at night, and they sleep most of them naked on the straw, and of course do all their occasions in their cribs.' At weekends they were chained hand and foot, with little food, and a patient described what happened on the Monday when the Keeper returned. 'I have seen them,' he said, 'in depth of winter, when the snow was on the ground, put into a tub of cold water and washed down with a mop.'

This was borne out by a discharged patient: 'They were washed in such a manner as would make tears come out of any Christian's eyes; they were taken to a tub where there was ice in cold, frosty weather, and there they stand by the side of the tub and are mopped down just the same as if they were mopping an animal.'

Lunatics, as the mentally afflicted had been called in law since the time of Henry VIII, were treated primarily as dangerous, to be kept in confinement. Watching the antics of idiots at Bedlam (Bethlehem Hospital) had been a pastime of Londoners, but the old Bedlam in the City had been pulled down and a new one built twelve years earlier in 1815, south of the river, where conditions were much improved. Yet strait-jackets, whips and chains were still believed to be the prime cures for madness. A humane method which treated the affliction as an illness had been applied by a Quaker in York and by French doctors, yet when the Committee asked a medical witness whether 'in the lunatic asylums in the neighbourhood of London any curative process is going on with regard to pauper patients', he replied: 'None at all.'

The distressing evidence convinced the Committee that earlier legislation had done little to improve the lot of lunatics. As witness after witness was examined, Ashley began to feel a strong desire to see with his own eyes, rather than sit listening in a committee room in the usual way. Seizing the opportunity of disputed evidence on a trivial matter he volunteered to visit the White House. On 27 June 1827 he rode through the city and out to Bethnal Green, then a semi-rural suburb.

'I well remember,' he told the House of Commons many years later, 'the sounds that assailed my ear and the sights that shocked my eye' as he went round 'that abode of the most wretched'. He was moved to the depths and returned home raging at the cruelty and pain; the sufferings of his fellow beings tore at his own nerves. Yet Dr. Warburton, who owned several other pauper madhouses and only visited the White House for one hour twice a week, was not a bad man at heart, merely struggling to earn his living. After the Select Committee's findings he put his affairs in order and spent liberally, until fifteen years later Ashley, who had watched him carefully, could publicly commend the improvement.

Following the Select Committee, its chairman brought in a Bill. He asked Ashley to second it, who thus made his maiden speech on 18 February 1828. It was almost inaudible to the press gallery but Sir Robert Peel told Lord Bathurst, who passed on the encouragement, that it was a good

speech and had only needed to be louder. 'And so,' wrote
Ashley that night in his diary, 'by God's blessing my first
effort has been for the advancement of human happiness.
May I improve hourly!'

During the debates on the County Asylum Bill and the
Madhouse Bill Ashley realised that he would have to intervene at length. Long before the day he felt nervous and
timid, and prayed 'most earnestly, as I ever do, for aid and
courage'. On 17 June his speech delighted the House. He
heard frequent cheers and received numerous compliments. 'I thanked God repeatedly – hastened home to
throw myself on my knees in gratitude.'

Both Bills became law and set up fifteen Metropolitan
Commissioners in Lunacy. Ashley became one, and the
following year he was appointed chairman, a position
which he held for fifty-seven years, apart from a brief break
towards the end of his life, when he resigned in protest at
some clauses in a Lunacy Bill, which then lapsed on a fall of
Government and he resumed the chair.

Even before he was chairman he had begun a practice of
regular visits to asylums, choosing a Sunday at first because
in unreformed houses the keepers 'sought their own
amusements and left the unhappy lunatics to pain and
filthiness'. He spent seven and a half hours at it on Sunday
10 July 1828, driven by a sense of duty to stoop into cells
where his stomach rebelled. He knew he had a long hard
task, visiting, attending commissioners' meetings, plan-
ning legislation, if the conditions of lunatics were to be
transformed. 'There is nothing poetical in this duty,' he
noted, 'but every sigh prevented and every pang subdued,
is a song of harmony to the heart.'

*   *   *

A few days before Ashley made his maiden speech he had
become a junior minister. The Duke of Wellington had
succeeded the feeble Goderich and had at once told Ashley
that he would require his services. The Duke put him in as
one of the Commissioners of the Board of Control, the

political masters of the East India Company which already
governed much of India. The salary seemed riches: Ashley
paid his debts, sent a handsome gift for the poor of the
parish to the rector of St. Giles, and subscribed to King's
College, which was being founded to uphold Christianity
in the new, secular London University.

The Board of Control opened fresh vistas to Ashley. He
conceived that the aim of Britain should be primarily the
welfare of the 'countless myriads' of India, as an integral
part of the British Empire, giving them the blessings of
good government and Christianity; he identified himself
with missionaries rather than merchants, though he kept
on warmest terms with directors of the East India
Company. When a pompous fellow-Commissioner urged
him to cut them socially he retorted in his diary: 'Stuff – if a
man be honest I am proud of his acquaintance. His recom-
mendations would lead me to treat them with vulgar
insolence. I shall not do so.'

He soon found that his colleagues in the Government
were irritated by his ideas. Lord Ellenborough, President of
the Board of Control for much of Ashley's time, wished to
be rid of him. When Ashley spent long hours composing a
despatch to the governor-general which would have
allowed Indians to sit on juries, Ellenborough rejected
it. Ashley's plan that the assistant to the Astronomer of
Bombay should be an Indian was also rejected. Nor was
Ashley good at defending or promoting in the House
any small matter which did not engage his heart.

One day the Board had before it the question of *suttee* –
the Hindu custom of burning widows on their husband's
pyres: ritual murders which were condoned by the British
for fear of riots. Ashley promptly remarked that *suttee* was
a 'most outrageous cruelty and wrong'.

The others turned on him. 'I was put down at once as if I
were a madman; I was wondered at for even daring to
mention such a thing.' However, Lord William Bentinck
was already on his way to India to be governor-general.
Appointed by Canning after five other men had refused the
post, which Wellington would never have offered,

Bentinck was an Evangelical whose wife was an ardent evangelist in her circle. The abolition of *suttee* was one of numerous reforms he hoped to make. Ashley not only encouraged him by letter but refused to sign an insulting despatch from the Board. In December 1829 Bentinck persuaded his reluctant council in Calcutta to decree the abolition of *suttee*. No riots followed. As Ashley commented in a speech long afterwards, 'The whole of India was satisfied because his Lordship appealed to those great principles of the human heart which are implanted by the hand of God.'

In the eyes of Wellington's entourage Ashley's two years at the India office did not enhance his career. They had expected him to be the next Prime Minister but three; instead he had proved somewhat unbiddable, though Wellington continued to befriend him. Nor was Ashley sure about the future. Frequent self-criticism made him doubt that he would ever reach the Cabinet, 'yet if I quit the service of politics, where are my means of utility?' After walking the cliffs near Brighton alone, praying and meditating, he could write: 'On my soul I believe I desire the welfare of mankind!' But work for India, like his support for the campaign to abolish slavery in the British Empire, was welfare at one remove.

Apart from his work for lunatics, which by its nature could only be a side-line, he was not yet fully engaged in 'the cause of the weak and those who had none to help them'.

4

MINNY

Lady Emily Cowper was the toast of the town in the season of 1828. Seventeen years old and very pretty, Minny's sunny nature made everyone happy. She also sang well: Queen Victoria some years later wrote that she had 'a really beautiful voice, so rich and full'.

Her legal father was kindly Earl Cowper but society gossip believed that she was really the daughter of Lord Palmerston: it never was proved and even her mother, the delightful but loose Countess Emily, Lord Melbourne's sister, may not have been sure. Lord Palmerston always treated Minny with special affection.

That summer of 1829 Ashley was desperate for a wife; apart from a desire for the happy home which he had never known, he was sure that only marriage could contain his strong sexual desires. From the break with 'Liebe' until her death, he had repressed them. Two months afterwards, at the opera, he had a most sudden feeling; 'it can hardly be called *love*; but sure enough a beautiful girl has made me dream of things that I had entirely forgotten since the days of my Antoinette.' The girl's name was Lady Selina Jenkinson, daughter of Lord Liverpool and niece of the late Prime Minister.

Ashley hoped to win her. He was serious, for he wrote to St. Giles's to enquire about his new little mare: 'Might I entrust her to carry a lady?' The agent, Gee, replied that she was gentle and quiet and that the groom was now getting her used 'to petticoats and an umbrella'. But Lord Liverpool discouraged the match, and soon Ashley was glad: he wanted not only beauty but a 'companion of my life and my mind'.

'Oh my prayer, my prayer, how I repeat it! A wife! a wife!' Several girls were amiable but none seemed right. Then his thoughts went to Minny Cowper: 'There is one that I know not well; she is lovely, accomplished, clever, with an almost virgin indifference towards her admirers.' She had already rejected or discouraged four, including Lord John Russell, the future Prime Minister.

But Minny's mother was a Lamb. Ashley summed up the Lambs neatly: 'A family which, gifted with talent and good humour, seems to confound the distinction between right and wrong.'

Then he recollected that his own sisters were not affected by the failings of their mother, from whom he was still estranged; and when he saw Minny again, on 2 August 1829, he fell in love. 'What a paradise of ecstasy it would be to share with this lovely girl all the sublimities of religion if she has a good and affectionate heart . . . There is something in her too fascinating.'

He followed the Cowpers to Tunbridge Wells and by August 11 was in little doubt that 'she is the woman whom God will give me as His choicest gift. I feel as though I could love her beyond the love of mortals. Oh, great God, what a treasure to possess such a darling!' Minny, however, was not sure. She prevaricated when he proposed in the street on their way to call on Princess Lieven. Ashley was upset. 'I became very angry and refused to enter Madame Lieven's house, she seemed alarmed and entreated me. I went. We walked home. I could not but admire her decision. It was so honest and unworldly.'

A few days later they all dined at the Lievens'. Ashley's cousin George Agar-Ellis noticed that he was 'evidently desperately in love with Emily Cowper', and was asked about him by her mother: 'She says her daughter does not care for him.'

Ashley, however, was making a strong impression on the family. Minny's brother William, then at Eton, told his

school friend George Leveson-Gower as they chatted at
Tunbridge Wells 'several anecdotes of the singular characteristic energy, earnestness and tenderness' which Ashley
showed 'in all the actions of life'. George (later second Earl
Granville) himself was impressed by him as a 'singularly
good looking man' with a striking presence. And not long
afterwards it seemed to be Countess Emily rather than her
daughter who was in love with the handsome, manly
Ashley. She could not make up her mind whether to
encourage the match. As her brother Melbourne was to
remark to Queen Victoria, 'My sister's fault is indecision
and irresolution.'

Ashley was invited to the Cowpers' family home,
Panshanger, near Hertford, in the autumn, but Minny
could not make up her mind. Then she refused him. On
October 29 Agar-Ellis recorded that 'Ashley is very low and
disconsolate about his rejected love for Lady Emily Cowper.' Nor were the respective families helpful. The Cowpers and Lambs were Whigs, the Shaftesburys Tories. 'An
odious father and four beggarly brothers,' thundered
Minny's uncle, Frederick Lamb, the British Ambassador
in Lisbon, to his sister. He pointed out that a third of
Ashley's income came from a ministerial office 'which he
will probably lose very shortly and which you and I both
devoutly hope that he may'. They would be poor. 'What
has poor Min done to deserve to be linked to such a fate,
and in a family generally disliked, reputed mad, and of
feelings, opinions, connections directly the reverse of all
of ours?'

Ashley's father was equally annoyed, since Minny had
no large fortune. Father and son had been briefly reconciled, then the earl was angry because Ashley disobeyed
him and voted with the Duke of Wellington for Catholic
Emancipation. Lord Shaftesbury spread tales against his
son. In January 1830 Ashley called on one of Minny's aunts
by marriage and begged her 'to clear him of the accusations
of tyranny, violence and moroseness, they charged him
with'. He may have been referring to Minny's relations but
his father could be the source, for at the time of the Reform

riots a year later, in rejecting a suggestion by his agent that
Ashley should raise and command a troop of yeomanry,
the earl wrote: 'His excessive irritability of temper would
give daily offence.' Yet the earl hardly ever saw his son.

Next month Lady Granville was writing to her sister
Georgiana, now Countess of Carlisle: 'Lord Ashley behaved most beautifully last night. How that girl can help
liking him, seeing his devotion to her, with something so
noble, so manly in his whole conduct! He danced all night
with the girls, did not follow her at all, and his spirits
appeared good without being forced, though I, who know,
could have cried over him.'

At last Minny gave in and they were publicly engaged. To
Lord John Russell it was Ashley who looked the more
love-struck. On her part 'it was not the sort of violent
passion which would not listen to reason,' so her uncle
Melbourne told the young Queen eight years later.

They were married at St. George's, Hanover Square on 10
June 1830. The earl stayed away on a flimsy excuse, but
almost immediately was 'thoroughly ashamed of his conduct', according to Lady Cowper, who was already
'Dearest Mum' to Ashley. The earl strutted about at Lord
Hertford's reception, accepting congratulations, and invited the Cowpers to dine, which they did, hoping to
promote reconciliation. Lady Cowper wrote to Ashley: 'The
world, and all who know you and Lord S. can have but one
opinion upon you both and upon your conduct to each
other – yours being everything that is good, and his everything that is bad . . . Odious as he is, we cannot prevent his
being your father or his having the power of annoying you
in various ways.' She helped to bring them together again –
until the next breach – and Minny delighted her crusty,
difficult father-in-law.

Ashley and Minny were at once blissfully happy. 'My
dearest love,' wrote Minny the first time they were parted,
when Ashley was standing for Dorchester in the General
Election which followed the death of King George, 'I really
am *quite* miserable without you. I would not have believed
that I should have minded so much your going away for

two days . . .' And she ended: 'There certainly never was such a darling as you are dearest Ashley and I really think I love you more every day. Good-bye darling, I shall be *so much* disappointed if you don't come.' On another occasion she wrote that nobody could be more happy than she at the return of 'her own darling Hub' except his dog Bobby, 'who has never known a moment's happiness since you went – he is always pacing up and down stairs and listens at the door with his little head cocked on one side. I never saw such a darling.' This was probably the Newfoundland dog, finely bred and of 'the small and sleek kind' (a variety now extinct) which Ashley had ordered as a puppy when they were engaged.

Whenever Ashley and Minny were parted they longed for each other. 'My own dearest Pet,' wrote Ashley during the Election of 1832 when he won the county seat, 'I admire and love still more and more such a sweet and darling and affectionate and honest a creature as you. God be praised who gave you to me.'

Minny's heart had been open from the first and she was soon (in Ashley's words long after) 'a sincere, sunny and gentle follower of our Lord', without losing her naturalness and high spirits. Their home reflected her sunny nature, and she could laugh at herself and at him. 'I don't know how it is,' she wrote, 'I not only love you but when you are away I *hate* everybody else.'

Their first child, Anthony ('Sir Babkins', then 'Accy') was born on 27 June 1831. However many they might have, Ashley was determined to make their childhood as happy as his own had been miserable. Minny could not have made a child unhappy had she tried.

Both doted on their baby, Minny 'without vanity as he is the image of you. Everybody who sees him is quite struck with the likeness.' He was the admiration of the town, she wrote later from Brighton, 'but he grows so wilful there is hardly any managing him. So *violent*. It is *astonishing how like his father he is*!! Good-bye darling.'

5

THE CRY OF THE CHILDREN

Early in February 1833, a day or two after the opening of the first Parliament to be elected since the Great Reform Bill, two gentlemen were shown into Ashley's study at 20 New Norfolk Street (now Duncannon Street) between Grosvenor Square and Hyde Park.

One of them was well known to him, Sir Andrew Agnew, a Scottish Member particularly interested in Sunday observance: Ashley had favoured the Bill he had brought in, which had lapsed when Parliament was dissolved. The other man was a stranger, whom Agnew introduced as the Reverend George Bull, a Yorkshireman. Agnew explained that Bull had been sent to London by a committee which was agitating for a reduction of the hours worked by children and young people in factories: ten hours a day should be the limit. A Ten Hours Bill had been introduced by Michael Sadler, a Yorkshire M.P., but he had been defeated in the General Election by Thomas Babington Macaulay, future historian, and the committee were looking for another Member to put the cry of the children before the House. Agnew was too busy with his Sunday Bill. Others had declined. Ashley's name was on the list which Bull had brought to London.

Ashley had only recently become aware of the conditions and inhuman hours of children who worked in mills and factories. Sadler's Bill had made little stir, and when it was before the House Ashley had been much distracted, not only by the Reform Bills, which he had opposed, but by his

fight for the county seat. While sitting for Dorchester he
had won a by-election for the much more important representation of Dorset against William Ponsonby, husband
of Ashley's first cousin, the fifth earl's daughter whom
Minny naughtily described as 'that nasty little woman Lady
Bab'. The great expense had fallen almost entirely on
Ashley; then Ponsonby had tried to unseat him on petition,
bringing more expense, worry and debt.

However, Ashley had lately read in *The Times* some
extracts from the evidence put before Sadler's Select Committee, and had been shocked. In most textile mills little
children were working impossible hours, often under
blows from overseers. They were denied education except
for some Sunday schooling in places, and many of them
died young or were crippled for life. Earlier Factory Acts
had scarcely touched their plight, which had been worsen-
ing for the past thirty years until the recent agitation led by
Sadler and others. As with negro slavery, nothing substantial could be done for the 'little white slaves' except by
Parliament.

When Sadler lost his seat in December 1832 Ashley had
written him a note offering to lay petitions on the Table or to
help in other small ways, but on receiving no reply he had
forgotten the matter: unlike Ashley's lunatics, Sadler's
factory children were far away in the north.

But now, on this February day, Parson Bull was pouring
out in graphic detail the horrors of the factory system.
Ashley's heart was touched. He loved children, and he was
specially upset that countless hundreds should be growing
up brutalised, without moral guidance or the help of
religion, to the lasting damage of the nation.

He saw at once that to accept leadership in such a cause
would bring labour, expense and pain, and would perhaps
damage the political career on which he was set. Nor was he
eloquent. 'I can perfectly recollect,' he wrote five years
later, 'my astonishment, and doubt, and terror at the
proposition.'

He asked Bull and Agnew to try others but they had
exhausted their list. He asked for time to reflect but Bull said

he must have an answer in twenty-four hours because Lord Morpeth (Ashley's college friend George Howard) was about to bring in a Bill to limit hours to eleven. This was not acceptable to the 'Short Time Committee' which Bull represented. Ten hours a day was their demand: even that would bear hard on younger children but a shorter period would allow a mill owner to use two shifts a day, and thus would increase the hours of the adult operatives whom the children assisted, and cause more children to be employed.

Agnew and Bull withdrew. Ashley consulted two fellow Members, who urged him to accept. He interviewed Bull again. Alone he thought it out, prayed for guidance and sought it from the Bible. Still undecided he went up to Minny, who was pregnant with their second child. He laid the whole question before her. She did not hesitate: 'It is your duty,' she said. 'Go forward, and to victory!'

Next day Bull returned for his answer. Ashley first praised Sadler's pioneering and then said: 'I have only zeal and good intentions to bring to this work. It seems no one else will undertake it, so I will. And without cant or hypocrisy, which I hate, I assure you I dare not refuse the request you have so earnestly pressed. I believe it is my duty to God and the poor, and I trust He will support me. Talk of trouble! What do we come to Parliament for?'

At half past two in the afternoon of 5 February 1833, he announced in the House that he would reintroduce Sadler's Bill and was loudly cheered, thus receiving no indication that a battle of fifteen years was about to begin. Bull listened from the gallery and wrote glowingly to the Short Time Committee in Bradford: 'As to Lord Ashley, he is noble, benevolent, and resolute in mind as he is manly in person.' And the poet Southey wrote to him: 'Thousands of thousands will bless you for taking up the cause of these poor children.'

A few days later Ashley addressed the London Society for the Improvement of the Condition of Factory Children. A royal duke was in the chair and Daniel O'Connell, the fiery Irish leader, newly elected to Parliament, sat among those on the platform.

Young Lord Ashley, nearly thirty-two years of age, stood erect and somewhat stiff, his hand on the rail, his thick dark curls carefully in place, his voice 'fine and rich in tone' but still a little inaudible at the back. As the prosperous audience listened, a trifle worried lest they be promoting revolution or, at the least, the economic collapse of the nation, Ashley told them that the Ten Hours issue was a 'great political, moral and religious question': political, because it would decide 'whether thousands would be left in discontent – aye, and just discontent'; moral, because 'the rising generation should learn to distinguish between good and evil' and be no longer degraded. And 'it was a great religious question; for it involved the means, to thousands and tens of thousands, of being brought up in the fear of the God who created them.'

Tribes who killed unwanted babies or sacrificed their children to Moloch were merciful, he said, compared with Englishmen of the nineteenth century; 'for we, having sucked out every energy of body and soul, tossed them on the world a mass of skin and bone, incapable of exertion, brutalized in their understandings, and disqualified for immortality.' All England now knew about this 'terrible system' and could not escape guilt if it continued.

Ashley was not an emotional speaker but his peroration was moving. 'I assure you,' he said, 'I will not give way a single moment on the question of the Ten Hours. I will persevere in the cause I have adopted. I took up the measure as a matter of conscience and as such I am determined to carry it through.

'If the House do not adopt the Bill they must drive me from it, as I will not concede a single step. I most positively declare that as long as I have a seat in that House, as long as God gives me health and a sound mind – no efforts, no exertions, shall be wanting on my part to establish the success of the measure.

'If defeated in the present Session I will bring it forward in the next! And so on in every succeeding Session until my success is complete!'

He sat down to great applause. The House of Commons,

however, leaned more towards mill owners, some of whom had entered Parliament after the Reform Bill and supported the Whig government. Several master spinners wished to lessen the children's hours but feared competitors, and were outnumbered by those who resented interference by Government. To gain time they petitioned for a Royal Commission of Enquiry, which was granted by one vote in a small House against Ashley's opposition.

Ashley declined on principle to give evidence; moreover he had no first-hand evidence to offer. He had set himself an 'invariable rule' to see conditions for himself, but during the Session he could not make the long journey to the north: the first line of railway out of London was still being planned. He had mastered the question from papers and interviews.

The Royal Commission went to work at once. Factory children, primed by agitators, danced round the three Commissioners, singing a jingle demanding the Bill; thus disclosing that some at least had energy left. The Short Time Committees often refused to co-operate. In Manchester they organised a monster march of children, straight from work and in filthy garments. Yet in spite of all difficulties the Commissioners produced their report with a speed which shook the masters. And the report admitted much of the case which Sadler and Ashley had made. It did not recommend all they wanted for young people but went further for the very young. It showed little interest in education or morals.

On 17 June 1833 the House gave a second reading to Ashley's Bill. He feared that the Government would seek to wreck it in Committee and wrote on 24 June to Lord Althorp, Earl Spencer's heir, who was the genial Leader of the House, to urge the *absolute necessity* of legislating during this Session'. He warned Althorp that 'unless we carry a satisfactory, and therefore a final, measure, the evil will be rendered ten fold more disastrous and alarming.' Any scheme to make young people between fourteen and eighteen work longer than ten hours a day would be 'stoutly, fiercely opposed' in the north.

Ashley did not make things worse by publishing private information that civil unrest might follow rejection of his Bill, and from the start he had told his Short Time friends that they must keep the peace and avoid violent language if they wanted his leadership; but he believed that the north of England was in a ferment and on 5 July, in committee, he defeated Althorp's delaying proposal to refer the matter to a Select Committee upstairs. Victory seemed in sight. Then, a fortnight later, the House considered the heart of Ashley's Ten Hours Bill, the clause which would extend protection to all under eighteen.

Led by Lord Althorp the House defeated the clause by a crushing majority of one hundred and forty-five votes. For all his fine words in February Ashley realised that he could not force the pace; yet he had so shamed a reluctant Whig Government that they could no longer ignore the question. He rose in his place and said: 'I find that the noble lord has completely defeated me. I will therefore surrender the Bill into the hands of the noble lord. But having taken it up with a view to do good to the class intended, I will only say, Into whatever hands it passes, God Bless it.'

Althorp soon produced a Bill which gave much to the children in the textile industry except the silk mills. Those under nine were not to work at all; those between nine and thirteen should work only eight hours, and some education should be provided. Inspectors should see that the new laws were enforced.

Ashley recognised that the Bill had value; but it fell short, might be evaded, and did not touch the mines or many other trades which exploited children. He must allow time to show both its value and its failures, and then try again.

On 29 August 1833 Althorp's Factory Act became law. One day previously, the Royal Assent had been given to the abolition of slavery in the British Empire, ending the long campaign begun nearly fifty years before by William Wilberforce, whose funeral Ashley had attended in Westminster Abbey on 6 August. Thus the two crusades and the lives of two great social reformers touched briefly and symbolically in August 1833, an end and a beginning.

6

TILL WE HAVE BUILT JERUSALEM

On a cold February day in 1836 Ashley's carriage turned off
Fleet Street and stopped in Salisbury Square. As he alighted
and entered the headquarters of the Church Missionary
Society his mind was full of a great plan, not this time
for the myriads of India but for the working classes of
England.

Althorp's Factory Act of 1833 was already proving defec-
tive, and Ashley could not forget the human misery which
was the price of Britain's rapidly expanding industrial
wealth. During Peel's short lived Conservative ministry of
1834–5 he had been Civil Lord of Admiralty (though hurt
that Peel had not offered a higher place) and the Ashleys
had lived in Admiralty House with its fine reception rooms
and beautiful balcony. Office prevented him introducing
further motions; moreover he knew that the Act must be
given a free trial; but he was determined to win shorter
hours for all factory operatives as soon as he could. Meanwhile he had become more and more convinced that the
deepest need of the people was spiritual.

All England had been divided into parishes since time
immemorial. The past two generations, however, had seen
sleepy villages become factory towns, often overpopulated
through the crowding together of shoddy houses and
tenements. In a few industrial parishes the vicar or rector
could afford one or more curates; in others the incumbent
was idle, or an absentee who put a poorly paid curate in his
place; but up and down the country, by the late eighteen-

thirties, were a growing number of earnest parsons who were trying to help and teach their people singlehanded, without means to pay for assistants. Thus thousands of parishioners in the poorest parts were scarcely touched by religion.

Methodists and other Nonconformists were doing much in some parts, and Ashley honoured them, unlike his parents and most of the aristocracy and bishops; but now and for the rest of his life it was his 'heartfelt and earnest desire to see the Church of England the Church of the nation, and especially of the very poorest classes, that she may dive into the recesses of human misery and bring out the wretched and ignorant sufferers to bask in the light and life and liberty of the Gospel.'

To this end he went by appointment to Salisbury Square to discuss with three or four friends a plan to raise money. As a result some sixty men, clergy and lay, met on 19 February 1836 in a larger room at Salisbury Square, with Ashley in the chair, and founded the Church Pastoral Aid Society 'for increasing the number of working clergymen in the Church of England, and encouraging the appointment of pious and discreet laymen as helpers to the clergy in duties not ministerial'.

The new Society was immediately attacked by the whole bench of bishops because their sanction had not been sought first. Some objected to the use of laymen; others did not, but feared that the C.P.A.S. would form a new order of teachers outside episcopal control. Ashley spent hours writing letters or calling upon bishops and churchmen, to smooth difficulties and remove misunderstandings. Thus he sought the support of the headmaster of Harrow, C. J. Longley, who refused it. A few months later Longley was consecrated bishop of the newly created see of Ripon, the first step on his path to Canterbury. He soon recognised the valuable aid which the C.P.A.S. had already brought to hard pressed clergy in Leeds and elsewhere and became a supporter. The energetic Bishop of London, Blomfield, a great builder of churches, also changed his mind but never gave public support.

Every year, according to Government papers, the movement of population from the countryside to the factory towns put a further 100,000 souls outside the reach of religious ministry. Ashley, appalled, sympathised with the desire of the early C.P.A.S. to finance lay helpers without limit, but he agreed with a compromise in 1837 that all such stipendiary laymen should be under the absolute control of an incumbent. This did not satisfy young W. E. Gladstone, who wished to limit lay assistants to those who were training for holy orders; he and some other vice-presidents resigned and founded the Additional Curates Society.

The breach was an early sign of the religious strife which was to be an unfortunate feature of Victorian England. Ashley's own cousin and contemporary at Christ Church, Edward Bouverie Pusey was one of the leaders of the new, and as yet very small, Oxford Movement whose Tracts for the Times (hence 'Tractarians' or 'Puseyites') seemed to the general public to urge a more Roman direction for the Church of England.

Ashley had an eye for religious art and was not against symbols; on a tour of the Continent he bought a small crucifix which 'does but simply recall His death and passion'; he liked to see the cross as part of the scenery in Catholic countries, and their open churches and the unashamed devotion of the people. But he hated superstition and was deeply suspicious of any movement which seemed to place priests between the people and God, or would reverse the Reformation. He was especially against the loudly expressed political ambitions of the Roman Church.

He loved the liturgy of the Church of England and deplored any misuse. When Minny's sixth baby, Lionel, was christened at St. George's, Hanover Square, in October 1838 Ashley was most disappointed because the service was 'abominably performed by the curate Mr. Scholefield; hurried over with the utmost indifference of voice and manner – never looked at the book, examined his nails, picked his ears, dressed his whiskers, surveyed the people, etc. etc. while he vomited the prayers – five hundred such men as he would drive half the congregations to the dissenting Chapels.'

Instead of worthless Scholefields Ashley wanted good men in reasonably sized parishes: 'I would assign to every 3000 souls a resident pastor with a decent income and a comfortable house,' and let him do his work without interference from the State. The Church Pastoral Aid Society was a means to that end, and after its early difficulties it went from strength to strength.

Every year the annual meeting in the newly built Exeter Hall would bring together a large body of the subscribers who made pastoral aid possible. Ashley invariably took the chair, as president, and he would bring with him an array of M.P.s and peers for the platform, including on one occasion his eleven-year-old cousin, the Duke of Marlborough's heir. Unfortunately Blandford grew up to be the centre of a scandal; but for many others their support of the C.P.A.S. helped them to live as unashamed Christians. As Ashley once pointed out, in his boyhood most of the aristocracy were cold and contemptuous towards religion but already many were warm and sincere.

Ashley's speeches at the C.P.A.S. were widely reported, to be read in rectories and manor houses and humble homes throughout the kingdom, and by clergy and laymen whom the Society helped. It was these who proved its worth. The C.P.A.S. was an important factor in the quickening increase of religious faith in England. 'We can quote very great and unmerited success,' Ashley told the fifteenth annual meeting, but this only emphasised the summits ahead.

*　　*　　*

In these years of the eighteen-thirties Ashley's personal religion went deeper, with a strong sense of the presence of God, even when afflicted by the depressions which seem to have been part of the Ashley Cooper inheritance. His favourite Bible verses were those on the theme: 'I will never leave thee nor forsake thee,' or Christ's own promise to the disciples, 'Lo, I am with you always.'

One strong influence was friendship, begun in 1835, with a former secretary of the Church Missionary Society, Edward Bickersteth, who was rector of Watton, near Hertford, where Ashley stayed (and was 'a great favourite' with the children). Bickersteth, then aged forty-nine, was a noted Evangelical author, compiler and hymn writer, with an interest in the Early Fathers and in Anglican liturgy. The two men found they had much in common.

Bickersteth had recently changed his views concerning the Second Coming of Christ. Recent generations had almost forgotten the Advent hope of the Christian Church, 'He shall come again in glory, to judge both the quick and the dead.' Christ's own warnings, and the conviction of the Early Church that they should expect Him, had been replaced by a vague belief that He would not come again to establish His reign of peace and bliss until all the world had been saved: a doctrine of no comfort to Ashley, surrounded by the miseries of the factory children, the lunatics, the pauper blind and a growing number of 'those who had none to help them'. As Bickersteth unfolded the Scriptures and lent him recent books which had reconsidered the subject, Ashley's heart leaped to think that Christ would come again suddenly and soon. Since Christ Himself spoke of understanding the 'signs of the times', and referred His disciples to the prophets of old, Ashley began to delight in the study of prophecy. The motive of all he did was unchanged: the love of Christ, and Christ's love for man. But Ashley more than ever wished to be found faithful and ready if Christ should suddenly return, and the last verse of the Bible became his prayer: 'Behold I come quickly . . . Even so, Come Lord Jesus.'

The study of prophecy in the context of the times became of great interest to both Ashley and Minny. 'My dear Rabbi,' runs one letter to a learned friend, 'I and my wife are very anxious to have a good "prophetical" talk; would you come and dine with us on Wednesday or Thursday?' The 'Rabbi' was an Irish Protestant, the Reverend Alexander

M'Caul, D.D., a Hebrew scholar who had thrown up the prospect of a brilliant academic career to work among the Jews of Warsaw as agent of the London Society for Promoting Christianity among the Jews. He was now settled in London, and when Ashley's interest in prophecy determined him to learn Hebrew, so that he could read the Old Testament in the original as fluently as he could the New he had turned to M'Caul.

Reading the Old Testament gave Ashley a concern for the Jewish people; study of prophecy convinced him that they would return to the Holy Land, now an almost barren waste after centuries of Turkish rule. In April 1839, following correspondence with the British Foreign Secretary, Palmerston, Lord Ashley wrote an anonymous article in the *Quarterly Review* advocating, in effect, a Jewish national home in Palestine, with Jerusalem its capital, under Turkish rule but British protection. Later he drafted a formal letter to Palmerston which M'Caul's daughter copied out on gilt-edged creamlaid paper for presentation.

The times were ripe, for the Great Powers were heavily involved in the 'Eastern Question', with Britain and Prussia supporting the Sultan of Turkey and France his rebellious vassal, Mehemet Ali. Politics and religion coincided, and since Palmerston had recently married Minny's widowed mother, Ashley was well placed. Palmerston, a jaunty pagan who cared nothing for religion, was fond of Minny's husband and glad to forward his scheme since it fitted his diplomatic and military ambitions for the Levant. Moreover, Jews throughout the Turkish empire would then look to England for protection.

The next step was to create a Protestant bishopric of Jerusalem, jointly sponsored and supported by England and Prussia. The Lutheran King Frederick William favoured it; religion and statecraft coincided again. The bishopric plan became a veritable hobby-horse for Ashley and when he learned that the King of Prussia was coming to England on a State visit he was so beside himself with joy that even Minny was exasperated: 'You din this perpetually in my ears, and it sets my back up against it, always talking

of "how wonderful, how wonderful,"' mimicking his rais-
ing his eyes to heaven. The two made it up very quickly; it
was at this very time that Lady Lyttleton commented after
they had dined at Windsor: 'He is very fond of her and she
of him, and it is always pretty to see his awfully handsome
face soften whenever his eye meets hers.'

The King of Prussia, a tall, fat man who looked and talked
like a good-natured farmer, but had piercing eyes, received
Ashley and his friends graciously and invited him to select
the first bishop. M'Caul refused, saying it should be a
Christian of the Hebrew race; therefore Michael Alexander,
a learned convert, was consecrated by the Archbishop of
Canterbury and sailed in a British warship.

Bishop Alexander died in Jerusalem less than three years
later. His successor was a nonentity. This first bishopric of
Jerusalem survived for nearly fifty years, but was of little
consequence, and the scheme for a Jewish homeland came
to nothing. But 'Lord Shaftesbury's vision' is enshrined in
Israeli history as having inspired the first steps towards the
return of the Jews to Palestine.

And Bishop Alexander sent Ashley a ring made by
Jewish craftsmen in Jerusalem, engraved in Hebrew letters
with a verse from the Psalms: 'Oh, pray for the peace of
Jerusalem; they shall prosper that love thee.' Ashley wore it
for the rest of his life.

*   *   *

Neither Ashley's distant vision for the Jews nor his far flung
plans for pastoral aid in England could weaken his resolve
to relieve immediate distress.

In the spring of 1840, standing in the half light of early
morning at a window at the back of his house in Upper
Brook Street, where they had moved in 1833, he noticed in
the mews a small boy, with face and ragged clothes filthy
with soot, his limbs twisted and his back bent beneath a
bundle of rods and brushes, and beside him a hulk of
a man who cuffed him as they walked back from work
– the chimney sweep and his climbing boy. Ashley knew

that the boy did not merely carry the rods. He went
naked up the chimneys, crooked, narrow and rough, to
dislodge the soot.

In the sweep's wretched warren, as Ashley later discovered, the boy was prepared for his work by being
rubbed all over with salt water in front of a hot fire – an
excruciating process – to harden the skin. His knees and
elbows were often grazed as he climbed, and when he stuck
his master lit a fire of straw to induce him to struggle
violently enough to free himself: boys sometimes suffo-
cated. He was often so terrified that a beating was the only
way to make him work. 'All children want a deal of coaxing
or driving at first,' said a friendly sweep, 'though I should
be as kind as I could, you must ill-treat him somehow.'
Many of them died from a peculiarly painful cancer.

The horrors of chimney climbing had been known to the
public since 1785, when the eccentric character who invented the collapsible umbrella had written a book expos-
ing the use of the boys, but nothing effective had been
done – it all happened when honest men were asleep; few
ever saw a climbing boy, and their masters often locked
them up on Sundays so that no one should notice their
misery. Machines had been invented to render boy sweeps
unnecessary, more books had been written, victims had
died and Acts of Parliament passed. An Act of 1834 was due
for renewal and a fresh Bill had already been promoted.
Ashley supported it strongly, unearthing evidence and
frustrating several wrecking amendments.

'My hands,' he lamented in his diary on 1 July, 'are too
full, Jews, Chimney-sweeps, Factory Children, Church
Extension, etc., etc., I shall succeed I fear, partially in all,
and completely in none. Yet we must persevere; there is
hope.'

The Climbing Boys Bill became law in August 1840,
but the housewives of England rose up in arms to make
it a dead letter; thirty-five years would pass before the
Shaftesbury Act of 1875 finally abolished the practice of
sending boys up chimneys.

Meanwhile Ashley was trying to rescue the boy he had

seen. He sought out the master and offered money to buy out the apprenticeship. The master haggled for more. Ashley put the matter in the hands of Robert Stevens, an insurance man and secretary of the society campaigning for abolition. Stevens tracked down the boy's father and on Ashley's behalf offered him free education for his son, who was described as of gentle and sweet disposition.

At length the father agreed, 'and to-day,' recorded Ashley on 19 September with a flourish, 'the child will be conveyed from his soot-hole to the Union School on Norwood Hill where, under God's blessing and especial, merciful grace, he will be trained in the knowledge and love and faith of our common Lord and Saviour Jesus Christ.'

7

THE HORROR OF THE MINES

The young Queen Victoria was writing up her journal after giving a party at Buckingham Palace on 8 December 1837: 'Lady Ashley was looking quite lovely . . . After dinner I sat on a sofa with Lady Ashley who was very agreeable and talked to me of her children etc. One of her charms is being so natural.' Afterwards the Queen's beloved Prime Minister, Melbourne, 'spoke to me of Ashley as a very good man, and less eager in politics than when I first came to the throne'.

As Lord Melbourne's niece, Minny and her husband were frequently invited by the Queen. Once, as they all were going into dinner, Melbourne murmured, 'There goes the greatest Jacobin in your dominions!' They all laughed, but Ashley was sure that Melbourne regarded him as too revolutionary; and when the Queen and her minister were discussing him, Melbourne spoke of Ashley as 'being very anxious to ameliorate the suffering of factory children, which Lord Melbourne thinks very doubtful. If they don't work they must starve, and the greatest philanthropists only wish to reduce the number of hours of work from fourteen to ten; but then the manufacturers say they will be ruined and that they cannot compete with the Continent.' On another occasion, speaking of the Ashleys' 'happiness together', Melbourne spoke of 'his being of a fidgety temper but she managed him very well'. Ashley was never at his ease with Melbourne, who in male company larded his speech with blasphemies without even noticing.

The Queen much enjoyed Minny's company: 'Such a nice amiable person,' though dreadfully frightened when invited to sing. The Queen had the Ashleys and their two older boys, Anthony and Francis, to stay at Windsor. Her lady in waiting, Sarah Lady Lyttleton, wrote to her family: 'They are a very interesting *ménage* to watch. A very sensible and most highly principled man, full of useful good qualities, having married his beautiful wife and taught her all the good she could not learn from her mother. So that, from being a flirting, unpromising girl, she is grown a nice happy wife and mother. Her manner is perfectly unaffected and good-humoured – not, however, to me a very pleasant one; but it is pleasant to see her in every sense.

'Then their two eldest boys are very dear creatures, seven and five years old, most lovely to behold in their green velvet frocks and long, perfumed hair. Their beauty is most striking; and not wonderful, considering both parents. And they are all spirits and naturalness, and so tractable and well trained! The Queen had them to play with her for an hour in the corridor Saturday, and I quite enjoyed it. They had neither Nurse nor Mamma with them, and were most funny and good, throwing great balls at us, and then screaming, "*Queen!* Look, I have killed the Lady!" Having first declined playing at ball – "I don't think it right *in a palace*; I might hurt something" – and talking with such spirits of "lessons with Papa, reading, and saying by heart". I am glad to have made acquaintance with the family; it is pleasant to think about.'

When the 'Bedchamber Question' arose on the fall of Melbourne in 1839, it was Ashley whom Peel took to the Palace in hope of persuading the Queen to replace some of her Whig ladies. Ashley had complained to his Whig mother-in-law, at the start of the reign, that Melbourne should have allowed some Tory ladies in the Household. Peel now found the Queen's mind fixed, and Ashley never left the carriage. Peel then gave up the attempt to form a government, and Ashley was at least relieved that he would not now be a ministerial member of the Household, having only accepted such a low place in the intended

ministry because Peel almost burst into tears when he tried
to refuse. Melbourne was therefore in power when the
Queen married Prince Albert; she wanted no Tories at her
wedding but grudgingly agreed to ask five, including the
Duke of Wellington and the Ashleys, though she cancelled
a dinner invitation when Ashley abstained in the vote on
Albert's allowance and precedence, which the Government
lost.

Ashley could move with ease in the Palace and in the
great houses. He was also beginning to move easily in
slums, walking dark alleys or the streets with open drains,
as he accompanied clergy who were receiving help from the
Church Pastoral Aid Society. He also discovered the lay
missionaries of the London City Mission, founded in 1835
by David Nasmith, who had already founded missions in
Glasgow and elsewhere but died young. As Ashley
walked, with rather stately pace but no trace of condescension or aloofness, it grieved him to see the hordes of
ragamuffins, and he wondered how he could win them
education and opportunity.

His love for small children became all the deeper when he
was separated from most of his own during a holiday with
Minny and Accy, aged eight, in the north and Scotland. His
sister, Lady Charlotte Lyster, was looking after the five
younger 'kids' at Rowton Castle in Shropshire and Ashley
missed them sorely. 'Those darlings Edy and Mice [nick-
names for Evelyn and Maurice] are ever before me, and I
feel, every hour, the very absence from the five blessed
Chicks that God has given me. It shortens and attenuates
the pleasure of any journey.'

They had all left London that August of 1839 by the newly
opened railway. 'How our notions are elevated! Here we
are complaining that we did not, in our speed, exceed
twenty miles an hour; and that the journey which used
to occupy *twelve* hours had to-day occupied *six* hours.'
Charlotte Lyster remarked that 'the Devil, if he travelled,
would go by the train: immense speed, stink and uproar!'

After saying goodbye to her and the 'kids' at
Birmingham, Ashley, Emily and Accy 'spanked along the

railroad' to Liverpool. Here 'thousands of the dirtiest, worst clad children I ever saw, throng the streets, presenting a strange inconsistency with the signs of luxury all around. You marvel whence they come, until you get a peep into the side alleys, which are filthy and stinking, and crammed with beastliness like common sewers.' He realised that 'these cheerful but unclean beings' were children of the Irish who thronged into Liverpool to work the docks and excavate land for railway lines.

The railway went no farther than Preston: the Ashleys' long tour must continue by horse and carriage, beginning with the Lake District where it was nothing but 'rain, rain, rain'. After watching the pretty country children he wrote in his diary: 'I feel a sympathy and a love for the whole infantine world.'

The new railways were opening up the north as they spread their tentacles across the countryside in the next few years. Ashley was able to visit mills and factories bad and good, meet children crippled at work ('a whole alphabet' of deformities) and study all sides of the question. Investigation by itself could relieve neither child nor adult, but Ashley had secured the appointment of a Parliamentary Select Committee under his chairmanship to examine the working of the 1833 Factory Act; and, in August 1840, a Royal Commission on the conditions of employment of children in industries which the Act had not touched.

And thus, on 7 May 1842, Members of Parliament, and later the public, were shocked and disgusted by a volume which lay on their breakfast tables.

The Commissioners had chosen to visit the coal-mines first, and so appalling were their discoveries that the Home Office had tried to prevent publication of their report: 'It came,' said Ashley, 'by a most providential mistake, into the hands of Members.'

The sober text was illustrated by drawings on the spot, and men who had hitherto dismissed Ashley as a crank found their stomachs turning as they studied the pages; enormities which they fondly believed unthinkable in England were being perpetuated in mines belonging to noble lords and cultured men of fashion. Girls, almost naked and chained to heavy carts, drawing coals up low, narrow passages far underground; girls working alongside naked men, who sometimes sexually abused them. Children of five or even younger incarcerated without light, to work trap-doors in the rat-infested mines; children standing all day ankle-deep in water at the pumps. Hours were twelve or fourteen a day, six days a week. Sometimes children were kept underground night and day. Brutal overseers continually used a strap or even pick-handles to punish and oppress. 'My boy, ten years old,' one woman deposed on oath, 'was at work; his toe was cut off by a blind falling; notwithstanding this, the loader made him work until the end of the day, although in great pain.'

The sensation was enormous. The conscience of the nation was aroused. Ashley put down a motion to introduce a Colliery Bill releasing children and women from slavery in the mines. Peel's Government tried to edge him out. 'No assistance, no sympathy,' Ashley wrote of them, 'every obstacle in my way, though I doubt whether they will dare openly to oppose me on the Bill itself . . . God, go before us, as in Thy pillar of cloud.'

On the day allotted for his Bill, Ashley was forced by a trick to give way to another matter. 'Never did I pass such an evening; expecting, for six hours, without food or drink, to be called on at any moment – very unwell in consequence.' Another day was given, but an attempted assassination of the Queen caused the adjournment of Parliament. 'These repeated delays,' wrote Ashley in his diary, 'have tried my patience, and stumbled my faith – God forgive me.'

At last, a month after the publication of the report, Ashley rose in the House of Commons to introduce his Bill. The House, sitting in its gloomy temporary Chamber, the old Court of Requests which flanked Westminster Hall on the south, was packed.

'As I stood at the table, and just before I opened my mouth, the words of God came forcibly to my mind, "Only be strong and of good courage . . ."'

8

'I CANNOT FEEL BY HALVES'

The House heard Ashley in deepening silence as he disclosed what was happening to children and women down the mines. Some Members wept.

Ashley reached his peroration: 'Is it not enough to announce these things to an assembly of Christian men and British gentlemen? For twenty millions of money you purchased the liberation of the negro; and it was a blessed deed. You may, this night, by a cheap and harmless vote, invigorate the hearts of thousands of your country people, enable them to walk in newness of life, to enter on the enjoyment of their inherited freedom, and avail themselves (if they will accept them) of the opportunities of virtue, of morality and of religion.'

With a few more words he sat down, to tumultuous cheering from all sides of the House. Richard Cobden, founder of the Anti-Corn Law League, who publicly and bitterly opposed Ashley's factory reforms because the House would not 'untax the people's bread', and had described him privately as 'that aristocratic and canting simpleton,' came over and sat down beside him. Cobden wrung Ashley's hand and said: 'You know how opposed I have been to your views. But I don't think I have ever been put into such a frame of mind in the whole course of my life, as I have been by your speech.'

Prince Albert sent Ashley a warm message from the Queen and invited him to call; the newspapers, so often critical, praised him; the House of Commons passed his Bill with commendable speed. At first he could find no peer to introduce it into the Upper House, until the Earl of Devon obliged. The peers weakened the Bill before sending it back but by early August 1842, nine years almost to the day since the abolition of slavery in the British Empire, Parliament abolished the 'slavery' of women and children in the mines of Britain.

The awakening of a 'healthy and vigorous public opinion' enabled Ashley to revive hopes of a speedy end to overlong hours in factories and mills. His hope was to see 'the restoration of content among all classes – the revival of good-will between master and man – a blessing on every house, and a home for every labourer.'

The Royal Commission proceeded next to study whether children in employment were getting the education, brief as it was, which the Act of 1833 enjoined. They found that little had been done, despite the efforts of some voluntary societies. Children were growing up both illiterate and pagan. Ashley wrote to a friend in January 1843: 'The state of things is far more awful than I thought could be proved.' Without a strong moral and religious basis in society, no reforms could truly help the nation. On 28 February he therefore made a strong speech in the House on a motion for a Humble Address praying for 'instant and serious consideration' of the best means of diffusing 'the benefits and blessings of a moral and religious education among the working classes'.

In a long speech he put before the House the evidence gathered by the Commissioners, and pleaded that public opinion was ready for a great step forward; if the Government would insist that every employer of children and young people should arrange time for their education, the voluntary societies and the Churches would supply it. The resulting Government Bill, however, foundered on the disagreements of the Churches. Thus education of the poor became yet another of Ashley's unfinished crusades, another banner which he could not lay down.

He was more successful in his work for lunatics. For sixteen years he had been serving their cause as a tireless chairman of the Metropolitan Commissioners. In 1842 the Commissioners' powers of investigation had been extended to cover all England and Wales and they found the treatment of lunatics outside London to be generally deplorable, despite the fine work of the Quaker Tukes in York, and others, and of a few county asylums such as Surrey's: most counties left pauper lunatics to the mercies of private keepers who wanted profit. On 23 July 1844 Ashley brought the Commissioners' report before the House in another long and notable speech which made no concession to Members' feelings. He urged legislation 'on behalf of the most helpless, if not the most afflicted, portion of the human race'.

During the debate an Irish Member, Richard Sheil, the dramatist, who had opposed Ashley's Factory Education Bill the previous year, concluded his speech by saying, to cheers, that it did their hearts good to hear the noble lord. 'There is something of a *sursum corda* in all that the noble lord says.' ('This,' noted Ashley in his diary, 'is the most agreeable language of praise I have ever received. It is the very style I have aimed at.') 'Whatever opinion we may entertain of some of his views,' continued Sheil, 'however we may regard certain of his crotchets, there is one point in which we all concur – namely that this conduct is worthy of the highest praise for the motive by which he is actuated, and for the sentiments by which he is inspired.' Sheil added, with a neat allusion to the third earl's famous book, 'It may be truly stated that he has added nobility to the name of Ashley, and that he has made Humanity one of "Shaftesbury's Characteristics".'

Ashley was quite overwhelmed by the cheering from all sides. A year later he was able to put through Parliament the Lunacy Acts of 1845, 'the Magna Carta of the Liberties of the Insane,' which compelled every county to build an asylum and established humane attitudes and treatment throughout England and Wales.

*　　*　　*

Within three years Ashley had delivered children and
women from virtual slavery in the mines and brought
humanity to lunatics; but he was still unable to win the ten
hours' relief for young people whose overlong hours, day
after day for six days a week, were rotting their souls and
stunting their bodies. He was opposed by factory and mill
owners; by Cobden, Bright and the Anti-Corn Law League;
by economists and newspapers; by Peel and his Government, which Ashley had declined to join at its formation.

The haughty and unpopular Home Secretary, Sir James
Graham, introduced a Factory Bill which, in Ashley's view,
granted too little relief. Ashley brought in an amendment in
committee which would have secured a reduction to ten
hours, and to his joy he won it by eight votes. Peel and
Graham persuaded the House to reverse the vote by
threatening resignation, and smothered Ashley's hopes.

Despite plaudits like Sheil's, Ashley sometimes felt that
every hand was against him except that of 'the great unwashed'. 'Talk of the dangerous classes,' he once burst out
in his diary, 'the dangerous classes in England are not the
people! The dangerous classes are the lazy ecclesiastics, of
whom there are thousands, and the rich who do no good
with their money! . . . I am as much fretted by anxiety as
worn by labour. I cannot feel by halves, nor only when the
evil is present. I take it I suffer very often much more than
the people do themselves!'

His diary became his safety valve. Just as, a century later
in the Second World War, the imperturbable Field Marshal
Alanbrooke never showed irritation or discourtesy however much Churchill might exasperate as they hammered
out strategy, and then went home to explode into the pages
of his diary, so did Ashley. By the time he was in his forties
Ashley's public self-control was a byword, with courtesy
and charm and friendliness to opponents, though he could
be imperious and betray anger on occasion. Only Minny
knew the cost, in emotional turbulence and nervous ten-
sion, of his increasing warfare for 'the poor and those who
have none to help them' – only Minny and his diary.

He wrote his diary in the sight of God. He poured

out thanksgivings; often he wrote complaints like the
Psalmist's, 'Lord, how are they increased that trouble
me!', especially when he was gloomy for the future or
engulfed in the depressions which were a characteristic of
the Shaftesbury line. In 1867 he decided that he would
destroy the volumes of diary before the end of his life, or
have them destroyed by his executors. He pointed out in a
memorandum that his jottings were on the impulse or
information of the moment: he might correct facts or
change hasty opinions the very next day; many entries
would be misunderstood unless he were there to explain.

But he did not destroy his diary, except for certain pages.
In the last years of his life he reluctantly allowed Edwin
Hodder, his official biographer to study it.

Within a year of his death, therefore, the world was
astonished to read severe strictures and violent judgments.
His nephew apologised to Queen Victoria for comments
nearly fifty years old on Melbourne's likely effect on her
character. Gladstone considered that Hodder had been
reckless in the use of passages about living people, including himself. Gladstone's own diary was kept from his
official biographer, who was only allowed copies of
selected extracts. The Gladstone diaries, which proved
even more surprising than Shaftesbury's, were not published until long after his generation had gone.

Ashley generally wrote up his diary in the morning,
possibly as part of his preparation for the day, together with
prayer and reading the Bible. The diary helped his balance.
He could love a man (except perhaps Peel, whom he held
to have betrayed the factory children) while hating
'pernicious' opinions or actions. When dining or discussing, Ashley genuinely sought the good of guest or
host, and enjoyed his company however much they contended. Next morning, the diary open, the fellow's politics,
social blindness or religious heresy came to the forefront. In
the diary, and by prayer, Ashley purged his soul of any
bitterness, disgust or anger; and thus was ready to meet
him again in charity.

Published too soon, the Shaftesbury diaries misled

writers such as the Fabian economic historians J. L. and Barbara Hammond, who approved his reforms but rejected religion, into portraying a gloomy, grim and strait-laced figure; not the warm hearted Ashley, with wide interests and a strong sense of humour, whose face, with his blue eyes and curiously hooded eyelids, could look mournful in repose but light up with a wonderful smile: a man whom others delighted to serve.

*   *   *

When Ashley had taken up the Ten Hours question his sponsors had pointed out encouragingly that no one would accuse him of self-interest, for he represented a southern agricultural constituency. But as the years passed the opponents of the Ten Hours Bills had used this very fact to claim that his efforts were insincere: they said he attacked northern industry to protect southern agriculture. Again and again they cried that the needs of the poor in mill or factory would not be relieved by Factory Acts but by repealing the Corn Laws. Since 1815 the Corn Laws had kept up the price of bread by taxing foreign corn. The bad harvests of the eighteen-forties in England had brought more hunger because there was less home grown.

Ashley felt the force of the argument, but he had been a strong believer in Protection, and had been elected by farmers and landowners and other freeholders of Dorset to maintain it.

Another taunt was thrown at his head: the deplorable conditions on the Shaftesbury estate at Wimborne St. Giles.[1] Ashley felt this even more strongly because he had long deplored tumbledown cottages, poor sanitation and low wages in Dorset yet had no power to redress them while his father lived.

Then a Government commissioner reported adversely on the county. This gave Ashley his opportunity. At the

1. The mansion is St. Giles's House. Shaftesbury generally referred to it as The Saint, and the estate, village and church as St. Giles's.

sleepy market town of Sturminster Newton, with its fine
stone bridge over the swift-flowing Stour, he took the chair
at the agricultural society's dinner one November night. In
his pocket he had headings and notes carefully prepared,
and when the farmers and squires had fed well, and Earl
Grosvenor had proposed his health, drunk with acclama-
tion, Ashley stood up to deliver a courteously worded,
friendly, but strong request that they should consider the
recent charges.

'Do we admit the assertion that the wages of labour in
these parts are scandalously low?' he asked. If so, 'not an
hour should be lost in rolling away the reproach . . .

'Do we deny that the dwellings of the poor are oftentimes
ruinous, filthy, contracted, illdrained, ill-ventilated, and so
situated as to be productive of many forms of disease and
immorality?' If not, 'let us hasten to wipe out the stain;
the remedy is within our reach.'

He discussed the whole deplorable state of agricultural
conditions ('I ought not to be lynx-eyed to the misconduct
of manufacturers, and blind to the faults of landowners!')
and suggested that when his hearers sat as Poor Law
Guardians and cried out, 'Sluts and profligates!' after hearing long lists of bastardy cases, they should not assume that
'when in early life these persons have been treated as swine
they are afterwards to walk with the dignity of Christians.'

He pleaded for the farm labourer: 'Respect his feelings,
respect his rights, pay him in solid money' – and not in
'truck' (liquor or goods), which was one of the worst abuses
because it encouraged drunkenness and prevented saving.

'Throw open your gates, throw them wide open to the
poor, the fatherless and the widow.'

By the time he sat down he had his hearers right with
him. He had been ready to forfeit friendships but they
cheered him to the echo. Good landlords like Grosvenor
resolved to be even better; the hard hearted or mean,
whether squire or farmer, promised themselves to do
something some day.

Old Lord Shaftesbury read the speech in the papers and
was furious. Four years earlier father and son had been

reconciled, and the Ashleys and their 'kids' and nurse-maids were to spend a long Christmas visit at 'The Saint'. On the evening of 11 December, after the ladies had withdrawn and the port was on the table, the earl broke out in icy fury. Veiling his anger and avoiding violent gestures he accused Ashley to his face: 'You are exciting the people! You are inducing them to make extortionate demands! Once they are up they are not easily put down. They get on very well, I don't know how, at seven or even six shillings a week. You lack experience!' It was easy to point at the evil state of the cottages but he could not afford to improve them. Ashley, silent before the onslaught, reflected that his father had lately spent nearly a thousand pounds on a new hothouse. And the earl, now in his seventies, was granting long farm leases to disreputable men.

The one-sided quarrel made Ashley ill, yet he tried to love his father. 'God be with him,' he prayed, 'Open his eyes and touch his heart.'

On Christmas morning Ashley rose very early for prayer. 'Ah, blessed God, how many in the mills and factories have risen at four, on this day even, to toil and suffering!'

The next Christmas the Ashleys were not welcome at The Saint – 'turned out of my father's house' – and were warmly received instead by the Palmerstons at Broadlands, near Romsey.

The old earl's hatred could not affect Ashley's crusade for the children and young people – and their parents – in the mills; but the Anti-Corn Law League, with its cry, 'Untax the bread of the poor,' continued to strengthen resistance to the Ten Hours reform. And as the years of the 'Hungry Forties' wore on, with increasing distress in England and the approach of famine in Ireland, Ashley began to accept that the Anti-Corn Law League was right. Like the Whig leader Lord John Russell, and Sir Robert Peel the Tory Prime Minister, Ashley was converted to the Repeal of the Corn Laws; this would allow free trade in foreign corn, though to lessen distress in agricultural counties he wished it to be gradual.

But Ashley had been elected as a Protectionist and his

supporters in the county of Dorset would not changed their
views. He therefore decided that his only honourable
course was to resign his seat. 'What a tremendous sacrifice!
The Ten Hours Bill abandoned, and all my projects at once
extinguished.'

On 29 January 1846 he introduced the Ten Hours Bill
again. Two days later he applied for the Chiltern
Hundreds, leaving the passage of the Bill in other hands,
yet unable to keep away from the lobbies, or to have it out of
his mind night or day. In May the Bill failed again, by ten
votes. Soon afterwards, in June 1846, Sir Robert Peel re-
pealed the Corn Laws and was cast out of office by the fury
of his party; in the fluid state of politics Lord John Russell
was able to form a Government without a General Election.

That winter Ashley toured the north, addressing enthusiastic meetings in favour of Ten Hours: 'I must labour
and urge and compel, as though I were in Parliament and
the measure would be called by my name.' It was reintro-
duced by John Fielden, master cotton spinner and Radical
M.P. Economic and political factors favoured it at last, and
by the summer of 1847 the Ten Hours Bill had reached the
Statute Book, though there were unforeseen hazards
ahead.

Two months later, in the General Election, Ashley returned again to Parliament as Member for Bath.

9

THE WORLD OF OLIVER TWIST

A few years earlier Ashley had been reading *The Times* when his eye fell on an advertisement headed 'Ragged Schools'. Written from a street in a notoriously rough area of Holborn, north-west of the City, it invited the help of 'any lady or gentleman willing to assist as teachers'. The pupils were children and adults too ragged to enter a school; few dared enter a church. They were being taught free on Sunday and Thursday evenings by volunteers, and the effect on their lives was marked.

Ashley wrote off at once to this Field Lane Ragged School: he had been praying and puzzling for years about the illiterates of the slums. A day later a deputation of teachers called. Shortly afterwards he visited the school, a borrowed room in an area where policemen would only go in numbers, often carrying cutlasses.

Ragged Schools were springing up in other parts, mostly begun by missionaries of the London City Mission, though the patron saint was a crippled cobbler of Portsmouth, John Pound, who had taught 'waifs and strays' as he mended or made his shoes.

In 1844 the volunteers formed a Ragged School Union with Ashley as chairman, later to be called president. Of all the numerous causes he espoused, the Ragged School Union remained perhaps closest to his heart. Soon it was reaching hundreds, then thousands, of vagabond, thieving boys and girls from the stinking slums which were close behind 'the deceptive frontages of our larger thoroughfares', where sumptuous carriages trotted by, their rich and often kindly owners blissfully blind to the horrors which lurked so near.

It was the world of *Oliver Twist*, lately disclosed by Charles Dickens, though many of his readers declined to believe that he revealed fact. Ashley already knew that the truth was worse than even Dickens could describe, and in 1846–47, when out of Parliament, he went systematically over the worst parts of London, escorted by Dr. Southwood Smith, the sanitary reformer, and each district missionary of the London City Mission. As he wrote in the *Quarterly Review* (all articles were anonymous) he found children: '. . . in squalid and half-naked groups at the entrances of narrow fetid courts and alleys . . . The foul and dismal passages are thronged with children of both sexes, and of every age from three to thirteen. Though wan and haggard, they are singularly vivacious, and engaged in every sort of occupation but that which would be beneficial to themselves and creditable to the neighbourhood. Their appearance is wild; matted hair, disgusting filth, barbarian freedom from all restraint . . . Visit these regions in summer and you are overwhelmed by the exhalations; visit them in winter and you are shocked by the spectacle of hundreds shivering . . . all but naked.'

The horrors and misery weighed on him, kept him awake at nights and, despite his faith, deepened the natural streak of melancholy in his character. He was now in his mid-forties and his face began to be lined with suffering. He went on, even when his stomach turned. In the roughest areas he never received an insult. Until he became well known from prints, and received the deference due to a lord, the poor supposed this tall gentleman to be a sanitary official. They would gather round and he would listen gravely as they told him their grievances – bad water, open drains, crumbling overcrowded homes. He delighted in their irrepressible cockney humour. Children took to him instinctively. The City missionaries said that Lord Ashley could hardly bear to pass a ragged child without wanting to stop and talk.

Convinced that the Ragged Schools were one of the best means for helping children and adults to climb out of the gutter and to find faith, Ashley gave himself without stint. He advised the Ragged School Union committee and secretaries, he encouraged teachers, reassured clergy, gave simple talks to the children at their school anniversaries and was always ready to speak at a drawing-room meeting to beg support for a new school.

For the third Annual Meeting in May 1847 Ashley drummed up the Bishop of Norwich (Stanley) – the only prelate not afraid of meeting dissenters – Minny's brother, William Cowper, and the Reverend Baptist Noel, an earl's brother who was a fiery evangelist and popular preacher and had lately resigned his Holy Orders to become a Nonconformist. Ashley began his speech with a quip: 'Having lost those two letters, M.P., at the end of my name – so pleasing, so soothing and so influential – I feel quite satisfied with supplying the letters C.R.S.U., Chairman of the Ragged School Union; the public will probably sustain no loss by such a step!'

Back in Parliament he continued to give time to Ragged Schools despite his heavy political programme. A particularly bad slum had grown up in Westminster, close to the Abbey and the walls of the new Houses of Parliament which were rising from the ashes of the old. A missionary named Walker worked this district; but, as one of his colleagues wrote: 'The thickly-packed thousands who lived together in squalor, crime, and wretchedness resisted all efforts for their upraising, and were bitterly hostile to visitors who sought their good. Walker, after facing danger and assault for some time, gained a footing in this rookery, and found an old stable which he wished to convert into a Mission Room and Ragged School. Hearing of this, his Lordship, one afternoon, thoroughly visited the neighbourhood with the Missionary, and then, entering the House of Commons, collected from hon. gentlemen the required sum (£30) and sent it to Walker in the morning. This led to an increase of effort on behalf of the wretched inhabitants, with most satisfactory results.'

It amused Shaftesbury in later life to recall the day he had stood in the Members' Lobby as a beggar, hat in hand, collecting sovereigns or half sovereigns from friendly M.P.s.

He was also amused by the experience of an Old Bailey sessions judge, Joseph Payne, whose witty speeches were enjoyed equally by the boys and girls and their Ragged School supporters. Judge Payne went to inspect a new school (this was a few years later) and found 'only one or two lamps burning, all the windows broken, two of the teachers covered with mud from head to foot; the master was lying on his back, with six boys sitting on him, singing "Pop goes the weasel".' Ashley would remark that these were 'necessary preliminaries'.

The Ragged Schools meant as much to Ashley as he did to them. In a tough district with a high criminal element, south of the river, a missionary named Roger Miller discovered so many dirty, shoeless children clamouring to join his Ragged School that he needed larger premises. Ashley invited him to Upper Brook Street, then raised the money and visited the neighbourhood. They became firm friends.

Miller was killed in 1846 in one of the earlier railway disasters. Ashley promptly secured adequate compensation for the widow and orphans, and publicly lamented his personal loss. He never forgot Roger Miller. 'He was a humble, lowly man,' he would say, 'and poorly dressed, but I loved him for the excellent spirit that was in him; and he was blessed to my spiritual advancement. I could speak to that man with confidence; and then his sudden death led me to a more full dedication of myself to God and His poor.'

In 1848 the Ragged Schools proved their worth. Even Ashley dreaded a blood-bath in England when the fall of Louis Philippe, the French King, sparked off the 'Year of Revolutions' across Europe. London prepared for Chartist riots. Special Constables were sworn in by the thousands and Ashley found himself paired off with the exiled Prince Louis Napoleon, beginning a friendship which proved useful to his causes when the prince became Napoleon III. They were stationed in Fleet Street, and much amused at a working man's answer to their question about a peaceful rabble turning up a sidestreet: 'It's the revolution going down Fetter Lane!'

No revolution shook England, and Ashley always gave a large share of the credit to the past ten years' work of missionaries and clergy in the slums; the realm was saved by 'the influence of the Word of God'. Had there been, he would claim boldly, no London City Mission, Ragged Schools or Church Pastoral Aid, England would have suffered 'political trouble and convulsion' like the rest of Europe where buildings burned, men and women died and sovereigns lost their crowns. Perceptive statesmen agreed. Ashley once recalled how Guizot, Louis Philippe's (Protestant) premier, when a refugee in England, 'remarked to me "The religion alone of your country has saved you from revolution." This opinion was to a great extent endorsed by Sir George Grey, then Secretary of State for the Home Department, who in talking to me on the event, ascribed the good order, the peace, and high bearing of the people of the metropolis, to the oral and ennobling agencies that had been so long and so vigorously at work among them.'

Queen Victoria recognised Ashley's part in saving her throne. Nine days after the Chartist scare he was summoned to Osborne in the Isle of Wight, where the Queen and Prince Albert had built their country home. He asked Minny's brother to deputise at a Ragged School meeting and took the railway to Portsmouth where a royal yacht waited. At dinner he found the Queen 'very amiable and very considerate for the poor'. She told him they had sent for him 'to have your opinion on what we should do in the state of affairs to show our interest in the working classes, and you are the only man who can advise us.'

That night she wrote in her journal: 'Had some talk with Lord Ashley about the state of the working classes in which he takes such an interest. He said there existed the best disposition among them all, they only needed some comforts and some improvements to render their dwellings more healthy. No Charter was wished for, only sympathy and kind feeling, but if what had happened in France and

Germany had taken place here ten years ago, he could not have answered for the safety of the Empire.'

Next morning Prince Albert, who like the Queen was then nearly twenty-nine, took Ashley for a long walk in the grounds. They talked for an hour and a half. Ashley first asked whether he should speak freely or observe Court form.

'For God's sake speak out freely,' replied the Prince.

Ashley then suggested that if the Prince put himself at the head of 'all social movements in art and science, especially as they bear on the poor', he could do more than if he were king because he was not restricted by constitutional forms; yet his presence would be virtually that of the Queen, and would show 'the interest of Royalty in the happiness of the kingdom'.

'What can I do?' said the Prince eagerly.

Ashley had a plan up his sleeve. Four years earlier he had founded the Labourers' Friend Society under Prince Albert's patronage, to help young country people who drifted into London looking for work, only to be fleeced by rapacious lodging house keepers, and often led into crime. The Society also helped to lodge Londoners who had been thrown on the streets by the destruction of their tenements to build new roads or railways, or for smart houses which they could not afford. By 1848 it was also trying to encourage better dwellings for the poor, and soon would change its name to the Society for Improving the Condition of the Labouring Classes.

The Society's fourth May Meeting was due in a few weeks. Ashley suggested that Prince Albert, as president, should take the chair and make a strong speech, having first visited some of the mean streets within yards of Exeter Hall.

The Prince agreed with enthusiasm. Ashley returned to London, but the Prime Minister, Lord John Russell, promptly vetoed the plan, saying that he feared a disturbance by Chartists who would infiltrate the hall. Ashley believed that Russell was moved by jealousy because he had not thought of the idea himself, though Russell, like Melbourne, cared little for the condition of the people.

Prince Albert regretted that he would not be able to

demonstrate the sincere interest of the Queen and himself,
but felt constitutionally bound to accept the Prime
Minister's advice. Ashley hurried to Buckingham Palace on
the Royal Family's return and urged the Prince to stand up
to Russell: 'This is a matter in which your Royal Highness is
perfectly free to act as you may please.' He stressed that
the Prince's judgment was as good as that of the Prime
Minister.

Russell gave way with a bad grace, and on 18 May 1848
the Prince and his entourage drove up to Exeter Hall in a
splendid procession of three carriages with the footmen in
their red liveries, on Ashley's particular advice, to be welcomed by cheering crowds from the nearby slums.

Escorted only by Ashley and an equerry, with one or two
policemen in their black top hats, blue tunics and white
pantaloons, and the parish dignitaries, the Prince walked
up mean streets and into courts and alleyways. Ashley took
him into house after miserable house, and he was received
with the utmost enthusiasm and respect.

They returned to the audience of upper and middle class
men and women waiting in Exeter Hall. Prince Albert made
a fine speech written by himself, using facts supplied by
Ashley, in which he urged the rich to help improve the
housing of the poor, with loans and land allotments; to
recognise that the 'interests of the classes are identical', and
that they could unite to the advantage of each.

The speech was widely reported. It shocked Russell and
the Whig ministry but opened the eyes and purses of
commercial and professional men of good will who had
been frightened or ignorant of the poor. Phrases from the
speech, and the story of the Prince touring the tenements,
were soon told far and wide in the worst back-streets.

From that time on, the poorest knew that the young
Queen and Prince cared, and could be loved and revered in
return.

10

HOPE ACROSS THE SEAS

Ashley, in that spring of 1848, was talking one evening with the superintendent of a Ragged School. In another room the rough, half-clad boys and girls laboriously learned their letters. The rain beat down outside and a flickering gaslight on the corner of the building threw dreary shadows across the muddy pavement.

In a few minutes the children would be back on the streets in the rain with nothing to look forward to but a night in their hovels, or under the arches of bridges; and another day of begging, earning a precarious living by selling matches – or thieving. Ashley and the superintendent could not forget that three fifths of the work of a Ragged School was nullified by the hopeless future of the boys and girls; work could be found for a few, but the rest continued to drift.

A few weeks later, on 6 June 1848, Ashley made a speech in Parliament: 'The proposition which I make to the Government is this: that the Government should agree to take every year from these schools a number of children; say 500 or 1,000 boys and the same number of girls – and transplant them at the public expense to Her Majesty's colonies. If you will hold out to these children, as a reward of good conduct, that which they desire – a removal from scenes which it is painful to contemplate, to others where they can enjoy their existence – you will make the children eager by good conduct to obtain such a boon.'

Two objects would be gained: the Ragged School

teachers would have rewards to offer; and the best of the children would be given the opportunity to 'walk in all the dignity of honest men and Christian citizens' in the new lands of Australia, New Zealand and Canada, where men cared nothing for a youth's background which in England was an effectual barrier to his rise; where hard work and thrift could bring honour and fortune.

Rather to Ashley's surprise the government gave £1,500.

The children were selected with care, and when they sailed in the emigrant ship Ashley went down to address them – a batch of newly scrubbed boys, dressed in neat though rough suits given them to replace their rags. They were looking awed and a trifle worried, on the edge of a long voyage and an unknown world.

Ashley rose. 'I see you now, my boys,' he began, 'probably for the last time. You are going to a land where much will depend upon yourselves as regards your future prosperity and success in life. The whole world is open to you.' He spoke of their new life, and reminded them of those who had helped them in England. He told them that 'however you may rise in society – and there is no reason why you should not rise,' they must always work, since 'Christianity is not a speculation, it is essentially practical.'

He ended with these words: 'Whatever your duty or circumstances may be, *never forget prayer*. You may rise to high stations. Whatever success you may meet with in this world – and we heartily wish you may meet with great success – still, my lads, never forget the greatest ambition of the Christian is to be a citizen of that City whose builder and maker is God; and though we may never meet together again on earth, may we all at last meet together there.'

In due time glowing reports filtered back which the May meeting always enjoyed. '"I should be much obliged to you"' – Ashley was reading from a letter of a 'respectable magistrate' in South Australia to the Ragged School Union's honorary agent – '"if you could procure me some of Lord Ashley's lads" – you see he treats me quite as a family man [the audience laughed delightedly, most of them knowing that he had six sons], he looks upon them as my own children.'

He read out another letter from a boy who had been rescued in Westminster by the worst thief of the district, disgusted by the mother's ill usage; a child so scraggy that Ashley had almost thought he could hold him in the palm of his hand. The boy had done remarkably well, and now wrote in a good hand from Adelaide about Aborigines and kangaroos and the good wages and rations he would get as a shepherd. 'Contrast his situation with that of hundreds and thousands who are here,' commented Ashley, as he urged the supporters to continue to work. The Government withdrew after a year, and Ashley had to turn to them and to his friends and relatives: his sister Charlotte Lyster, who had no children, was particularly generous.

Ashley received one poorly spelt letter which he kept. 'Most Noble Lord,' it ran. 'I arrived at port Adelade after a very plesant passage and am now in a very comfortable situation with very pious people. I like Australia very well . . . I think with persevience, I shall do much Better here than in England . . . Please to except the poor thanks of your obliged and thankful servant CAROLINE WALKER.' On the back of the letter, years later, he wrote, 'She went into service, behaved so well that her master gave her in marriage to his son. She became a considerable person in Australia and afterwards in India.'

The emigration scheme was not limited to children. Soon after his speech in the Commons Ashley met a notorious thief, and on the spur of the moment asked whether he, too, would emigrate if he had the chance. 'I should jump at it,' he replied.

Ashley wondered whether an adult scheme would work, and sought the advice of a City Missionary, Thomas Jackson, who had the confidence of most of the criminals in London. Soon afterwards he received a round-robin signed by forty discharged convicts, inviting him to a conference.

One summer's night he went to the East End, and was received with loud applause by the most extraordinary crowd he had ever seen – some four hundred criminals (no one had been admitted unless he could prove that he was a crook) from elegant blackmailers to rough, scarred half-savages. Though no one said so, a few murderers were probably among them.

The missionary invited Ashley to open the proceedings with prayer. The thieves and ex-convicts went to their knees and Ashley offered up well chosen prayers (he never publicly prayed *extempore*) and, he said afterwards, 'the most devout of congregations could not have surpassed them in stillness and external reverence.'

He then said a few words; but 'I was anxious to know what was the character of these thieves, some of them pickpockets, some shoplifters, others of the swell-mob, and exceedingly well dressed some of them were. Many, however, had no stockings and some had no shirts. I wanted to know the great departments of roguery; so the Missionary said: "His Lordship wants to know the particular character of the men here. You who live by burglary and the more serious crimes will go to the right, and the others will go to the left." About two hundred of the men at once rose and went to the right as confessed burglars and living by the greatest crimes.'

Ashley assured them that he wished to help, but that first he would like to know more about their activities. Several thereupon made speeches, 'and anything more curious, more graphic, more picturesque and more touching I never heard in my life.' They told him all.

They agreed that they would only too willingly emigrate. In a land where no questions were asked they could make good. 'But how are we to live till our next meeting?' said one of the men. 'We must either steal or die.' It seemed a hopeless question, for at best not many could be sent abroad. Jackson urged them 'to pray, as God could help them'. Ashley, devoted to Jackson, felt strong sympathy with the thief who thereupon rose and said, 'My Lord and *Gentlemen of the Jury*, prayer is very good, but it won't fill an empty stomach!'

They all wished to emigrate, and Ashley promised to

HOPE ACROSS THE SEAS

help. Then one of the burglars stood up. 'Will you,' he asked Lord Ashley, 'ever come back to see us again?'

'Yes,' replied Ashley, 'at any time and at any place whenever you shall send for me.' He heard a low, deep murmur of thanks.

Ashley returned to the West End and persuaded a banker to sponsor the Thieves' Emigration. Thirteen left for Canada within three months, and after a year nearly three hundred had either gone abroad or found settled employment, without crime, at home.

11

FRANCIS

'I took *six* children last night to a conjuror and a dance at Lady Ailesbury's for 12th Night,' wrote Minny to her mother, Lady Palmerston. 'They were much amused and so was I . . . They had snapdragon and a supper of chicken etc. and champagne!!'

Lady Ailesbury, the popular 'Maria Marchioness' with her flaxen wig lived a short distance from the Ashley home in Upper Brook Street. Ashley himself was probably at the House or visiting a Ragged School but would have been amused by all the details on his return.

Minny's undated letter gives a hint of the happy family life which was one of Ashley's great supports. He was adored by his children. Anthony ('Accy'), the heir, was a happy-go-lucky, rather idle and brainless boy, and great mutual affection could not disguise Ashley's disappointment. He watched over Accy almost too carefully, in the manner of Evangelical families of the day, and dreaded to see characteristics of the Lambs (or whatever was the true blood of Minny and her mother) coming out. After a carefully chosen preparatory school in the Isle of Wight had failed to improve him, Accy was sent to Rugby, where Crauford Tait, the future archbishop, carried on the Arnold tradition; Ashley had rejected Eton and had not even considered Harrow, which was in temporary decline until the removal of the headmaster, Christopher Wordsworth, to a canonry. Rugby did not improve Accy either, and in 1848 he was put into the Navy when nearly seventeen and sailed for the Australian station, though his parents could hardly bear to see him go.

Their second son, Francis,[1] was very different. After a brilliant career at preparatory school he went to Harrow, now under Vaughan, and like his father entered the sixth form before he was sixteen, but worked hard and was reckoned one of the best brains in the school, with a fine physique too. He was mature, and charming, and a strong Christian who was popular with the other boys and much admired for his exceptional character, yet no prig. During the holidays he was already almost his father's private secretary, 'my companion, my co-adjutor, nay half my very soul'. As Minny put it when all was over, 'He had the most gentle and loving spirit and it would be vain to say that the loss is not heart breaking; and to Ashley the greatest deprivation of sympathy, interest and affection; for he was almost as much interested as he is, in all the objects in which Ashley loves to work.'

Only one letter from Francis survives, in a copy at St. Giles's, written to his younger brother Evelyn, soon to follow him to Harrow: '. . . I am glad you like school. Do try and get on as well as you can: Get Mr. Middleton's good opinion: I find here especially, that a master's good opinion of one is invaluable. Remember me to Henry [a school friend] and tell him I am very glad he is beginning to study prophecy: he will find it's most interesting. I hope to go for my Exeat on Saturday. When will you come home – Never omit to say your prayers or read your Bible.' He finishes with messages to the staff of his old school.

On Saturday 19 May 1849 the Ashleys received an urgent note that Francis was seriously ill. They rushed to Harrow. His illness was plainly pleurisy but current medical practice tried the worst possible cure: frequent 'cupping' or

---

1. The Honourable Anthony Francis Ashley. Each son, like all the uncles, was given the first name of Anthony, unused except for the heir. Cropley Earl of Shaftesbury was determined that never again should the holder of the title not bear the Christian name of the great statesman who had been created first earl. Cropley's children and grandchildren used Ashley as their surname. The full Ashley-Cooper was revived by the ninth earl.

bleeding. Had his strength kept up he might have re-
covered, even without the drugs of a later age.

'May 21st. – Dearest Francis no better . . . Saw him after
he had slept: very feverish, thirsty; but calm, composed,
and cheerful. Blessed be God, he is easy and peaceful!
Asked me soon after my arrival to read the Bible. Did it
joyfully. Read the seventh of Revelation for the glories and
bliss of the other world, and the twenty-fourth of Matthew
for the present duties and occupations of this. Prepared
thus for either alternative of God's will. Then we prayed,
and were, I think, comforted. What a darling, tender, true,
zealous, and God-serving boy it is! Oh, that he may be
spared to us, not for our solace and enjoyment only, but for
the Lord's faith and fear! How often have I meditated on his
future aid and sympathy in all my thoughts and pursuits for
the good of mankind. But I must imitate the example of our
dear Lord, and say, "If it be possible: nevertheless, not my
will, but Thine be done!" . . .'

They stayed at Harrow, spending most of the time at his
bedside. Next day Ashley wrote in his diary, 'He knows his
danger, but he knows also his hope. Never have I seen such
a boy; though so young, and as the world goes, so innocent,
he is filled with a sense of sin and unworthiness; and his
only fears are those which spring from a sentiment that
"the joys of heaven are too glorious for one like him". Oh,
what a mercy it is, and what a consolation to us, that he is as
far from self-righteousness as the east is from the west!
Never have I known until now what I am possibly to lose.'

Francis said: 'Read to me about the forgiveness of sins.'
They then read, 'and talked much of the free and full mercy
of God in Christ Jesus.' To calm any fears, they urged him to
remember that God is love: 'Human love,' said Ashley, 'is
capable of great things. What then must be the depth and
height and intensity of Divine Love. Know nothing, think
of nothing but Jesus Christ and Him crucified.' Francis
kissed his father repeatedly and blessed his parents for
bringing him up to love God.

As the days passed, Francis turned a little better. Every

boy in the school seemed to ask after him. Francis smiled and said it was only because he was his father's son, but Ashley knew from Dr. Vaughan and the masters that all Harrow was quietened and distressed and longing for his recovery.

Ashley had to go up to London for unavoidable duties, but as the train puffed towards Euston his mind could cling to hopeful signs, and they continued after his return. On the Sunday Ashley attended school chapel 'and took Sacrament. 120 boys are communicants. Can *this* be without its fruits? Blessed Lord, water it by Thy Spirit. Why in my day, not only no boys (and there were many of *seventeen* and *eighteen*) took the Lord's Supper, but no one dreamed of it.' This reflected the great change coming over England.

Later that morning Francis had a relapse, with intense pain in his lungs, so that Sunday was a day of 'fearful and agonizing anxiety', but on the Monday he was much better, and the doctors talked of permanent improvement. Francis asked his father, as he sat by the bedside, for prayers of thanksgiving. Ashley read from the Bible too. He asked whether Francis was able to meditate as he lay there, and the boy replied: 'Oh, yes! But I have learned what a futile thing must be a deathbed repentance! I feel that I have been reconciled to God – but what could I have done, lying on this bed, to make my peace with Him, had I not been brought before to a knowledge of the Truth!'

Recovery was shortlived. On the Tuesday came a relapse so serious and devastating that when the school doctor came, Francis asked him for the truth. Doctor Hewlett, who had already told Ashley that he now believed Francis would die, answered that he was in extreme danger. Francis smiled, and said, 'Whatever is God's will is enough for *me*.'

After the doctor left, the Ashleys came in. Francis asked whether it was true he might die, and when his father confirmed this, Francis said: 'Come near to me, dear Papa.'

Ashley knelt at the bedside and Francis hugged and kissed him, and again thanked him for the way he had been brought up: 'To you I owe my salvation.' 'No! dearest boy,' replied Ashley 'it is to the grace of God.' 'But you were the instrument of it.'

On the Thursday 31 May, he again seemed so much better that his parents began to hope. He chatted about helping his father again – and seeing his brothers and sisters. Suddenly, at sunset, he collapsed and died while his parents stood amazed.

They buried him at Harrow, the whole school following him to his grave, his parents in a daze of grief yet joy. He had taken them to Heaven's gate; and they were comforted, as Minny wrote, that Francis was 'enjoying the blessed presence of his Maker and singing the praises of his Lord and Saviour'.

12

THE CHOLERA YEARS

Ashley's step lost its spring. He suffered roarings in the ears and his nerves were taut. Minny was six months pregnant (Cecil was born in August) and to add to their anxieties, their third son, Maurice, who had been retarded since babyhood, began to have epileptic fits. But it was no time to give way to sorrow, for these were the cholera years and Ashley was deeply involved.

For years he had been urging improvement in public health. He wanted underground sewers to replace open drains; a pure water supply for London and the great cities; open spaces; and the closing of stinking graveyards: there were eighty-eight within the square mile of the City of London. He knew how unhealthily the poor lived, and more than once had returned to Upper Brook Street 'with a considerable household of vermin upon my back'. Moreover he was convinced that crime flourished the most 'in all places where neglect and over-crowding squalor keep fostering together'. Though better conditions could not remake human hearts, the nation had to be persuaded (against the then current theory) to improve public health 'before we could hope to evangelise the people'.

In 1848 his old Oxford friend George Howard, Viscount Morpeth, had steered through Parliament a Public Health Act which set up a Central Board of Health. As the Cabinet minister responsible, Morpeth would be president, with two salaried full-time commissioners, and one part-time, unpaid. That September the Ashleys were enjoying a holiday in a cottage on Wigtown Bay in Scotland, lent by Lord Galloway, when a letter arrived from Morpeth asking Ashley to be the unpaid commissioner.

His first reaction was to 'shrink from it, trembling at the responsibility of the office, the hardness of the way and the consumption of time and strength already over taxed by many undertakings'. But the more he walked in Galloway's estate and played with the younger children on the sands, the more sure he became that this was a call to public duty and to help the Government 'to give effect to their most important and necessary measures for the social and moral advancement of the people'.

He wrote to Morpeth accepting. 'It will be no small gratification to me, after many years of political difference, to be at last associated with the friend of my youth in a labour for the happiness of the nation; and I shall humbly and heartily pray to Almighty God that it may please Him, for the sake of our blessed Redeemer, to prosper this work to the glory of His own name, and the permanent welfare of our beloved Country.'

He already knew his fellow commissioners, Edwin Chadwick, the vigorous pioneer of sanitary reform, and Dr. Southwood Smith, who had taken him on his first tour of the slums as far back as 1841. But before he could put any of their plans to Parliament an outbreak of cholera became a serious epidemic. Ashley and the others were unceasing in their efforts to direct medical and social relief and mitigate the consequences of the high death-rate: more than 14,000 people died of cholera in 1849 in London alone, and a total of 53,293 throughout Britain.

During the summer following Francis's death the disease suddenly spread more rapidly – through medical ignorance of its cause. Ashley and Chadwick were already members of a new Metropolitan Commission of Sewers. Pending the building of a main drainage system, which they were demanding against strong opposition from vested interests, they were covering in the open sewers wherever they could overcome local prejudice. But Chadwick insisted that all sewers be regularly flushed; and since many of them emptied into the Thames, a mass of cholera-infected excrement soon fouled the water which was London's main supply: medical science believed that cholera spread through infected air, not water. Deaths rose sharply. Then a young doctor offered evidence that cholera could be water-borne. The flushing stopped but it was too late. In one week of August 1849 more than a thousand Londoners died of cholera.

Ashley stayed in the capital when almost all London society had fled to the country, and at one point he was the only one of the three commissioners who was not sick or unable to carry on. He suffered ill health during these years and for a time had to walk with a large stick; but none of his family were infected by cholera, though a few years later, during the next epidemic, Minny's brother-in-law, Lord Jocelyn, an officer stationed at the Tower of London, felt so ill as he came off duty that he stopped at the Palmerstons' house in Piccadilly and was dead of cholera within hours.

What caused cholera would not be known for thirty-four years, but enlightened observers saw a connection between epidemics and insanitary conditions. The Board of Health pressed for legislation. Edwin Chadwick was full of detailed plans which Ashley brought before Parliament; but Chadwick was a tactless bore, already unpopular in the country as the author of the notorious Poor Law Act of 1834, and he stirred up opposition as easily as he drafted his eminently sensible reforms.

Morpeth then succeeded to the earldom of Carlisle and retired to a less onerous post in the Cabinet. His successor, Lord Seymour, the Duke of Somerset's heir, was a high handed snob (married to a noted beauty who had been a queen of fashion) who cared little for sewers and burial grounds and was adept at rubbing up the salaried commissioners and their officials the wrong way.

One summer's day Ashley took his fellow commissioners for a country expedition. They boarded the South Western railway at the recently opened Waterloo station and travelled to Farnham. They rambled all over Frensham and Thursley commons looking for springs and streams of pure

water to pipe to London; and found what they wanted.
Ashley 'confessed that God is bountiful, but will *man* be so?
It is overwhelming, heart-breaking, awful to reflect how
many thousands are deprived, in this *Christian* city, of the
prime requisite for health, comfort, decency, of an essential
prop and handmaid to morality!'

Man was not bountiful. As soon as Seymour heard of the
expedition (he had not bothered to attend the meeting
which planned it) he angrily said they were exceeding their
powers by acting without his permission.

His attitude was typical of the frustrations faced at the
Board of Health. Ashley, with pardonable pride, had
hoped to go down in history as the man who had put
through Parliament the Act to give London pure and ample
water, and another to close the overcrowded burial
grounds and buy land for spacious cemeteries outside the
built-up areas of London, such as Brompton, Highgate and
Kensal Green; and to be the Parliamentary architect of an
effective system of great underground sewers, carrying
London's filth to disappear where it could do no harm.

One by one the schemes were slowed up, then stopped
or weakened beyond recognition. Moreover the 'great unwashed' did not want to be scrubbed behind the ears.
When, after six years of labour, the Board was abolished in
favour of a ponderous Government department, and its
unpaid commissioner was thrown on one side 'like a piece
of lumber', *The Times* shed no tears: 'It was a perpetual
Saturday night, and Master John Bull was scrubbed and
rubbed and small tooth-combed till the tears ran into his
eyes, and his teeth chattered and his fists clenched themselves with worry and pain.'

Ashley did not give up. In Parliament and out of it he
continued to press for public health. The reforms came at
last: Londoners could drink pure piped water, enjoy safe
drainage and 'go to paradise by way of Kensal Green'; but
London would have been a healthy place years earlier, with
countless lives saved, if Ashley had been allowed his head.

13

'THEY REGARD ME AS AN ENEMY'

Employers had found a loophole in the Factory Acts. With the recovery of trade they wanted more labour. They began to work the children in relays, broken by useless intervals when those off the looms were pushed out on to the streets. Thus the masters did not keep them at the looms for more than the legal six and a half hours for children and ten for those under eighteen; yet had them on call for a wearying eleven or twelve. And the adults might be at work for fourteen: their hope of shorter hours to coincide with the children's had proved an illusion.

Factory inspectors had tried to stop the practice, but on 15 February 1850 they lost a test case in the courts. Baron Parke ruled that relays were legal, whatever the intentions of the framers of the Factory Acts. Ashley was appalled: The Ten Hours Act was nullified. 'The work to be done all over again; and I seventeen years older than when I began!'

The Home Secretary, Grey, brought in a Bill which would stop relays but abandoned ten hours in favour of eleven – the young people would therefore work at the looms longer then before. The Bill was sure to pass. But Ashley found that the employers were ready to compromise on ten and a half hours and to accept a legally enforced half-holiday on Saturdays; so that the full working week of the young would in the event be shorter than even the Ten Hours Act had granted. He approached the Home Secretary who was willing to bring in the necessary amendments. Ashley announced his decision to support them by writing to *The Times* before he had convinced the Short Time Committees of the north. He knew they would be angry: 'Expect from the manufacturing districts a storm of violence and hatred. I might have taken a more popular course, but I should have ruined the question – one more easy to myself, but far from *true* to the people.'

The storm was far worse than he had feared. Though some in the north supported him, a vociferous group repudiated him for 'deserting the cause' by 'base and deliberate treachery'. They hurled insults, publicly, privately and in the House. He was hurt. 'They forgot all my labour of love . . . I won for them *almost* everything, but for the loss of that very little, they regard me as an enemy.' He rose in the House on 6 June 1850 to say he was more than sure that his decision was in the best interests of the operatives. The House heard him with respect and silence. 'I may be permitted to state, solemnly, and before this august assembly, that I have sacrificed to them almost all that a public man holds dear, and now I have concluded by giving them that which I prize most of all – I have even sacrificed to them my reputation.'

While accepting the Government amendments Ashley tried to strengthen protection for children by proposing that all their work should be done between 6 a.m. and 6 p.m., but his amendment failed to pass the Commons or the Lords, and for some years yet there were children who were forced to hang around a factory until as late as ten at night. But the Act of 1850 gave the substance of victory, and the employers accepted it without sulks and equivocation. Less than eighteen months later Shaftesbury (as he had become) learned by his rapturous reception in Lancashire that operatives, their children and their employers were happy in the working of the Act. As its benefits spread and a new generation of children grew up uncrippled by overlong hours, Shaftesbury was their hero, a legend in his own lifetime.

*   *   *

That same summer of 1850 brought fury on Ashley's head from another quarter. The previous autumn, after nine years of the Penny Post being delivered on weekdays, the Post Office had decided to add Sunday collections and deliveries. Sorters, clerks and postmen begged Ashley to prevent this destruction of their day of rest. He failed, but on 30 May 1850, to his own surprise, he carried a resolution through the House in the teeth of the Government. Sunday posts stopped, and Ashley received letters 'of deep, earnest, grateful joy from postmasters and messengers, full of piety and prayer'.

But the newspapers and the merchants and all London and county society howled for his blood. 'Bigot, fool, fanatic, Puritan, are the mildest terms,' he noted, and the Government worked hard to rescind the vote.

Ashley, like his predecessors from Hannah More and Wilberforce, who urged that Sunday should be a true day of rest, was thinking of the working man. He was not against innocent amusements and he positively urged physical recreation, but he believed that a Saturday half-holiday should be provided for these. Just as Hannah More attacked Sunday balls because hairdressers would be forced to work on Sundays or lose their fashionable customers, so Ashley wanted no postman to walk wearily, after six days on his feet, the miles of country rounds (one man in Dorset did twenty-two miles a day) or along city pavements; no sorter to be up early and then feel too tired for the church which the postman would be unable to attend. And Sunday should be for the family.

Moreover Ashley and his fellow advocates believed that a weekly day of rest and worship was an integral component of a Christian State. Ashley held to the tradition which the generations had passed down since before the Norman Conquest, and which was enshrined in the laws of the land, that England (and all the United Kingdom) was a Christian realm. Gladstone had lately abandoned this view, writing a most involved book to explain his change. Ashley held to it; but whatever might be the theory, working men should not lose their day of rest and worship for the convenience of the leisured classes who could take a rest on any day they chose.

These and the mercantile classes won the day. After three weeks the Government managed to restart the Sunday post. Sorters were turned out of bed; postmen lugged their sacks, 'and all,' wrote Ashley sadly in his diary, 'because certain aristocratic people' would have lost 'their gossip in the country every Sunday morning'.

14

NEW BEGINNINGS

In December 1850 Ashley made a speech which contemporaries considered one of his greatest outside Parliament.

Pope Pius IX (Pio Nono) had carved up England into dioceses with territorial names by a Bull couched in terms which to most Englishmen came perilously near deposing Queen Victoria in intention. The deep seated folk fear of 'Popery', a legacy of 'Bloody Mary', the Spanish Armada and James II, seemed to rouse all England. The traditionally Roman Catholic families, headed by the Duke of Norfolk, hastily reaffirmed their allegience to the Queen.

To the age of Pope John XXIII and Pope John Paul II the excitement might seem excessive, but this was the age of the Papal States, a byword for repression and backwardness; of Pio Nono's reactionary ways, and of a Catholicism which persecuted 'heretics' and often refused the Bible to the laity. Moreover a number of Tractarian clergy had 'gone over to Rome'. When John Henry Newman became a Roman Catholic in 1845 he had parted from most of his friends, but clergy and laypeople had followed him later, the Church of Rome requiring them to abjure their Anglican past in abjectly penitential terms. Others seemed about to go. This strengthened the widespread conviction that Tractarianism must lead to Rome, even if Gladstone and the Bishop of Oxford stayed loyal to the Church of England.

A great and representative audience, entirely lay, gathered at a large hall near Lincoln's Inn, with Ashley in the chair, to protest against the 'Papal Aggression' and to reaffirm the great Reformation doctrines of Justification by Faith and the priesthood of all believers, whereby no clergy of the Church of England should claim to be priests in the Roman sense of standing between the people and God. Speaker after speaker was rapturously applauded. Then Ashley rose.

Ashley never indulged in personalities, nor would he attack Roman Catholic laymen; indeed he encouraged Caroline Chisolm, the 'Emigrant's Friend', and honoured the nuns and the Sisters of Charity who nursed and relieved the poor. He called on this meeting to stand firm for Protestant truth and to frustrate those who would return England as a nation to Rome. 'We do not stand here to ask for penal enactments . . . We will invade no rights of our fellow-subjects; but, by the blessing of God, *they shall not trample on ours*. We wage no war with the Roman Catholics of these realms but we wage interminable war against the Pope and his Cardinals.' But, said Ashley with humour, the Pope had so stirred up England that they could forgive him and propose a vote of thanks, 'with what I am sure he will prize above all things – a handsome edition of the polyglot Bible!'

He then turned to the greater danger as he saw it: the growth of 'Romanizing tendencies' in the Church, and urged the bishops to stop them. 'The laity love their Church, its decency, its simplicity of truth, its Gospel character . . . but that Church must continue to be Scriptural.' If it changed its character they must be ready to do as their forefathers had, 'disregarding everything but the confession of the Truth and the honour of Almighty God.'

He ended with a personal declaration and an apt allusion and sat down to deafening applause. 'The whole assembly enthusiastically rose to their feet,' runs a newspaper report, 'and the ladies joined in the vociferous cheering.' Ashley thought the audience could have remained cheering till midnight.

Before Christmas Ashley took a huge petition to Prince

Albert. They discussed Church matters for an hour and a half, with Ashley delighted at the Prince's zeal and perceptions. Next year, 1851, Lord John Russell rushed through Parliament the Ecclesiastical Titles Bill, which promptly became a dead letter: the titles stuck, but out of the ferment came the Protestant Alliance, to awaken and unite all those, in every country, who wished to preserve or advance the Reformation, and to help the persecuted. Ashley, now the leading Evangelical layman, became its president.

*   *   *

1851 brought the Great Exhibition.

When Prince Albert thought up the idea of an international exhibition of arts and sciences, Ashley's first reaction was unfavourable because the emphasis would be materialistic. His tendency was always to take the pessimistic view, though one of his favourite phrases, 'God be praised,' was freely used whenever fears proved false; and in fact the Great Exhibition in the 'Crystal Palace' specially erected in Hyde Park brought forward several of his causes.

A meeting of Ragged School leaders the previous autumn, under his chairmanship, had discussed how the Exhibition might promote the schools. They had reached no conclusion. Afterwards three of the voluntary teachers had been crossing Holborn arm in arm when one of them, John Macgregor, a young barrister who inevitably was nicknamed Rob Roy after the hero of Scott's novel, suddenly said: 'Why not make some of our boys into shoeblacks, to clean the foreigners' shoes?' He had seen shoeblack stands in American streets.

He wrote that night to Lord Ashley, who received the note next day, for mail in London was swift. He replied at once, 'Good idea,' and sent a subscription. By the time the Great Exhibition opened, twenty-five boys, proud in a special uniform and fully equipped, were established by official permission at strategic stations in the Exhibition grounds. By the final day they had cleaned 101,000 pairs of shoes.[1]

The idea caught on. Shoeblack brigades were formed in different parts of London and in provincial cities and towns. Former street arabs were lodged together, loaned uniforms and equipment; they kept their takings except for a fraction which they paid to their brigade organiser. They learned to be smart and efficient instead of roaming the streets picking up odd jobs or relying on theft. The shoe-black became a well known figure in Victorian streets and squares and many of the boys impressed their customers enough to be found employment.

The Great Exhibition, though dedicated to international peace and progress, nearly opened without a place for the Bible. Ashley heard that, 'A large proportion of the Exhibition was taken up with guns, cannons, torpedoes, everything that could annoy and desolate mankind,' but the British and Foreign Bible Society had been refused a stand because it was neither 'art' nor 'science'. Ashley, as a vice-president of the Society and a personal friend of Prince Albert, at once sought an audience.

The Prince maintained that the Bible Society had nothing to do with the Crystal Palace. They argued for over an hour. 'Putting aside the religious aspect,' said Ashley at last, 'I will put it before you from an intellectual point of view. I ask you whether it is not a wonderful proof of intellectual power that the Word of God has been translated into one hundred and seventy distinct languages, and two hundred and thirty dialects . . .' He warmed to this theme until the Prince said, 'You have proved your right to appear.' But the Exhibition commissioners thrust the stand, with one hundred and forty eight translations displayed, into a remote corner.

Four days after the opening of the Great Exhibition Ashley was waited upon by a high powered deputation to

1. A few months later, in February 1852, John Macgregor started the Lawyers' Prayer Union (now the Lawyers' Christian Fellowship). The present writer's great-grandfather, Lord Chief Baron Pollock, and grandfather, who was later Baron Pollock, were among the founder-members.

beg him, at the second time of asking, to accept the presidency of the Bible Society, vacant by the death of ancient Lord Bexley, a superannuated Chancellor of the Exchequer from the time of the Napoleonic wars; Wilberforce had said of him that if everybody was like Lord Bexley the world would be a very much better place but a very dull one. Ashley had hesitated because he might seem to monopolise the religious societies; he was delighted when the committee insisted, for he regarded the Bible Society as 'the greatest and noblest' of them all.

*   *   *

A few weeks later, very early in the morning of Sunday 1 June 1851 before the household was astir, a groom from St. Giles's hammered on the door of Lord Ashley's house in Upper Brook Street, and pulled at the bell until a tousled butler drew back the bolts. The electric telegraph did not yet reach rural Dorset and the groom had been sent up by the mail train with news that the 83-year-old earl was dangerously ill. Ashley caught the first train from the new terminus near Waterloo Bridge, wryly recalling that he had tried to stop Sunday trains.

During the journey he could reflect that his father had never been fully reconciled to him, nor could see the point of social reforms; he had even opposed the Lunacy Bill in the Lords. He was not irreligious, but as Ashley once remarked to Minny, his father was one of those who 'preached the Church up, and acted it down'. His mother, on the other hand, had shown affection in recent years.

When Ashley arrived at The Saint to find his father in a coma she was grateful for her son's gentleness and understanding. 'I thank God,' she was to write a few months later, 'that in my affliction he has blessed me with two such sons as yourself and son William.' William, John, Harriet Corry and her daughter were present the next morning at seven o'clock when the old earl died. Ashley, after an all night vigil, led them in prayer: 'Lord Jesus, receive his spirit.'

Ashley was now the seventh Earl of Shaftesbury, though to his intimates he continued to be 'Ashley' according to the custom of the peerage, and to Minny: waiting for the family to gather for the funeral he stole a kiss on 'the lips of darling Minny's bust, the bust of my precious wife in her youth and beauty, but just as beautiful to me now, though twenty years have past.'

He had inherited a landed estate in deplorable condition. It would only increase his debts though every good cause in the world would think him rich. He must add the duties of landowner and squire to all his other responsibilities. 'How can I, at fifty years of age, learn other things? Land, rent etc. etc. is as Arabic to me.' He did not know that the resident agent and bailiff, Waters, was a rogue.

The stuccoed mansion needed repair. Begun in 1650 and added to at different periods, it had spacious rooms, an imposing front, and a stream which flowed right beneath it underground, relic of an ancient moat, but his father had wasted large sums on hothouses and other follies while ignoring the crumbling structure. Shaftesbury refused to touch it until the cottages could be improved: 'I have passed my life in rating others for allowing rotten houses and immoral, unhealthy dwellings, and now I am come into an estate rife with abominations.' 'Inspected a few cottages,' he noted in his diary, 'filthy, close, indecent, unwholesome. But what can I do? I am half pauperised; the debts are endless; no money is payable for a whole year, and I am not a young man. Every sixpence I expend – and spend I must on many things – *is borrowed!*'; 'Shocking stage of cottages; stuffed like figs in a drum . . .'

Within six months he had scraped together sufficient to build the first of many new cottages, had restored and redecorated the church, which had looked like a disused ballroom, and found a Scripture reader for an outlying village to assist the rather lazy ministrations of the rector of St. Giles, Robert Moore, whom his father had presented to the living nearly thirty years before. When another living on the estate fell vacant he gave it to young Edward Henry Bickersteth, son of his old friend who had lately died:

young Bickersteth was a man of pastoral and evangelistic zeal, a future Bishop of Exeter.

Within a fortnight of his father's death Shaftesbury had ordered the tap room at the public houses to close each night at nine, as was his right as squire: though no teetotaller, he knew that unlimited hours (as the law then allowed) of swilling cider, gin and strong beer were a prime cause of impoverishment and sexual abuse. And he waged immediate war on 'truck' (the paying of wages in undervalue goods or in liquor) which several of the tenant farmers practised.

Part of the property was let to small life-tenants, over whom he had no control. 'Visited some cottages – thank God not mine,' runs a later entry. 'What griping, grasping, avaricious cruelty. These petty proprietors exact a five-fold rent for a thing in a five-fold inferior condition! Oh, if instead of one hundred thousand pounds to pay in debt I had the sum to expend, what good I might do!' He built a school and planned two more so that each of his villages should have one; and began evening classes in winter and a cricket club for the summer.

Back in London he looked at the family mansion in Grosvenor Square, Mayfair, held on a lease with eighteen years to run, and renewable; it had been left to his mother but she made it over.

His parents had preferred to live at Richmond and had not troubled to oversee the caretaking servants. 'The building itself is out of repair,' Shaftesbury told his mother, 'and the interior is so filthy that none but those who had been there from day to day would have consented to remain in it an hour.' It needed expenditure outside and inside, and the furniture was 'absolutely worthless'. Shaftesbury found the money to renovate it by selling the lease of his house in Upper Brook Street.

24 Grosvenor Square became his London home.

* * *

By succeeding to a peerage he vacated his seat in the House of Commons. Old Sir Robert Inglis rose to move the writ for the election of a new Member for Bath: 'I believe' he said, 'that I speak the sentiments of the House generally when I say that Lord Ashley should not be withdrawn from the first ranks of this assembly, the scene of his labours and his triumphs, without some parting expression of respect and regret.

'During the last fifteen years of Lord Ashley's Parliamentary life he has been emphatically the friend of the friendless. Every form of human suffering he has, in his place in this House – and especially every suffering connected with labour – sought to lighten, and in every way to ameliorate the moral, social, and religious condition of our fellow-subjects. And out of this House his exertions have been such as at first sight might have seemed incompatible with his duties here. But he found time for all; and when absent from his place on these benches he was enjoying no luxurious ease, but was seated in the chair of a Ragged School meeting, of a Scripture-reader's Association, or of a Young Man's Christian Institution.

'I will add no more than that the life of Lord Ashley, in and out of this House, had been consecrated, in the memorable inscription of the great Haller, *Christo in pauperibus*.'

Lord Ashley had recently piloted through the Commons a Bill to reform the inspection of lodging houses: Prince Albert had erected model lodging houses near the Great Exhibition, which encouraged a sympathetic hearing. Lord Shaftesbury would now introduce it to the Lords, thus having the rare experience of piloting a Bill through both Houses.

He took his seat in the newly opened chamber designed by Barry, with its splendid ceiling, but he found their lordships dreary, discouraging and unfeeling. Everything had to be done in a brief period with few present, most of them impatient to speak before the House emptied for dinner. 'I broke cover in a bit of humanity-mongering about chimney-sweepers. Found my voice; was well received; "thanked God, and took courage."'

His first major speech on a national question made a much stronger impression than he had expected, both on the House of Lords and the nation. 'My dearest Evelyn' wrote Minny to their boy at Harrow, 'Your Father was *very* much pleased with your nice thought of writing to him to-day and with what you said.

'His speech has really been a wonderful success. I hear of it in all ways and on all sides – and the greater Triumph is the admiration of those who say "Tho' I do not quite agree" etc., and I feel it in a religious sense a great thing, as those who wish to decry religious truth are fond of saying that Ashley can only speak at Exeter Hall where he is "Cock in his own dung hill." Now he has excited immense admiration and astonishment in the House of Lords, where neither side exactly liked his saying what he did, and where therefore he would be sincerely and critically judged, with the remaining thoughts of Exeter Hall in the minds of his judges.'

Part Two

Noble Earl
1851–1885

15

BISHOPMAKER

'*Nov. 1st 1852.* My Lord and Lady to The Queen's at Windsor Castle by 1 o'clock train to London from Ring-wood to stay till 3rd. *Nov. 3.* My Lord and Lady to London and on to St. Giles at ½ past seven. Miss Cuyler came and stayed till 8th. *Nov. 4.* Mr. Chadwick, Dr. Sutherland and Dr. Southwood Smith came and stayed till the 8th . . .'

The butler – or another member of the household – had found an unfinished folio visitors' book from the time of the fourth earl, the friend of Handel. In the manner of country houses it was put to use again despite being nearly a hundred years old. The butler was entering it up each day, and thus recorded an informal meeting of the Sanitary Commissioners. They all went back to London on 8 November, starting from St. Giles's in four carriages. They were delayed three hours on the road by a bridge giving way near Dorchester, where they would have taken the Great Western Railway branch line; presumably they used Dorchester instead of nearer stations in order to examine the earl's terrace houses and cottages which he had inherited in a poor state.

The journal soon recorded the lying in state of the Great Duke. '*Nov. 17th.* My Lady dined at the Countess Waldegrave's. My Lord dined with the Duchess of Suther-land and went to the Lying in State' – and was appalled, though the butler did not know it. 'What a monstrous misuse of splendour,' recorded Shaftesbury in his diary. 'It was fine, very fine, but hardly impressive; signs of mortality, but none of resurrection; much of a great man in his generation, but nothing of a great spirit in another; not a trace of religion, not a show of eternity.' Romish countries would have done it better.

'*Nov. 18.* My Lady went with Lady Palmerston to Lord Hertford's House in Piccadilly to see the funeral procession of the Duke of Wellington. My Lord went with Master Evelyn to St. James's Palace' – and 'saw it well, singularly well . . . Day *providentially*, yes *providentially* fine; it spared, I doubt not (and let us thank God) many a sickness and many an accident. Stupendously grand in troops and music.' It occurred to no one that the next funeral to attract such crowds would be Shaftesbury's own very different one thirty-three years later.

The butler's journal continued day by day. The following spring it recorded an unusual episode. '*May 7th 1853.* My Lord and Lady went to Luncheon at the Duchess of Sutherland to meet Mrs. Stowe [author of *Uncle Tom's Cabin*] – My Lord had some gentlemen to dinner . . . *May 12.* Mrs. Stowe and some others to dinner.' The butler's phrase 'some others' was a masterly understatement about a 'very successful dinner'. The luncheon given by the duchess at palatial Stafford House (now Lancaster House) had been followed by a large reception, with guests ranging from bishops and peers to tradespeople and Quakers, 'and the wives of all'. The Shaftesburys' dinner 'brought together the Archbishop of Canterbury and the Rev. Thomas Binney, a flaming Dissenter,' and Shaftesbury rejoiced 'as a peacemaker'. After dinner the Grosvenor Square house was crowded with clergy and Dissenters, editors, shopkeepers, lawyers, peers, 'all with their ladies. It was quite a happy family; and everyone was mightily pleased.'

Harriet Beecher Stowe won all hearts, and Shaftesbury chaired a great anti-slavery meeting four days later at Exeter Hall and was even, 'for a wonder', satisfied with his own speech. He took the lead in the great agitation in Britain against slavery in the southern states of America. A few years later Evelyn, down from Cambridge, went to see slavery in practice as his father's eyes and ears. He was impressed in spite of himself by the happiness of slaves on a model estate in marshy land where no white man, it was thought, could survive; but he was horrified by a slave auction.

Shaftesbury's activities in 1853 did not please the southerners, and he would quote with much merriment a cutting from a religious newspaper in the south: 'And who is this Earl of Shaftesbury? Some unknown lordling . . . It is a pity he does not look at home. Where was he when Lord Ashley was so nobly fighting for the Factory Bill and pleading for the English slave? We never even heard the name of Lord Shaftesbury *then*.'

The campaign for the abolition of slavery was only one of the continually growing number of Shaftesbury's overseas concerns; and he had plenty to do in home affairs: chimney sweeps, child beggars, lodging houses, ex-thieves' refuges, Ragged Schools – he recorded during the summer of 1853: 'My heart goes so completely into every question that I fret like one possessed.' He was much encouraged that 'The working of the Ten Hours Bill is peace, wealth and happiness, social order, and moral improvement.'

His eye ranged overseas almost as much. As an annual traveller on the Continent he helped Waldensians and other Protestant minorities in Roman Catholic countries, was an ardent proponent of Italian unity and the friend of Garibaldi. Farther afield, he was active in the deliberations of the Church Missionary Society, the foreign work of the Bible Society, and other missions. He had been vigorous in his condemnation of the Opium trade and of the Opium War with China. He had kept a close eye on British policy in India since his own period in office, and was quick to denounce injustice while approving the principle of the *Raj* for its opportunities of doing good to every inhabitant of the sub-continent. During the Indian Mutiny he was much criticised for a speech condemning a particular atrocity by the mutineers which had never occurred: in a rare lapse he had relied on an inaccurate report of a letter from the governor-general's wife. Later he intervened to ensure Factory Acts for India and to improve public health.

When the Crimean War began in 1854 he could have wished to banish both Russia and Turkey to the ends of the earth, but accepted the Government's view that war with Russia, to save Turkey, had become inevitable. The sufferings of the British troops in the Crimea through illness, inefficiency, corruption and lack of medical supplies, as much as through enemy action, brought Shaftesbury into close alliance with Florence Nightingale whom he had known for years and had encouraged when her parents had tried to stop her unlady-like interest in nursing. He persuaded the Government to despatch a Sanitary Commission to the Crimea and Scutari, probably drafting the instructions himself from her notes. Florence Nightingale said afterwards that it had saved the British Army.

Before that, however, the Crimean War had brought Shaftesbury to one of the main painful decisions of his career.

At the height of the war the ministry fell and Lord Palmerston accepted the Queen's commission to form a government. He wanted Shaftesbury in the Cabinet to give it tone, and as Minny's stepfather to provide the Shaftesburys with the income which they deserved after selfless service. Shaftesbury decided to refuse because his reforming work might be stifled: in his diary he wrote himself into a frenzy of suspicion that Palmerston had been persuaded by men with this very purpose; but Minny, with wifely ambition for her oft-abused husband, and an understandable vanity, besought him to accept. Palmerston was not finding the formation of a Cabinet easy; the national crisis was urgent. At last Shaftesbury, overruled by the importunities of Minny, wrote a long letter of acceptance, reserving the right to vote against the Government in certain matters. Before the letter was sent, the Prime Minister withdrew the offer. 'Your Papa,' wrote Minny to Evelyn, 'has remained without an office, owing to the avidity of the Whigs, who would not allow Ld P. to admit anybody into the Cabinet who was not one of themselves. I own I regret it, but perhaps bye and bye we may see *why* it has been ordered so.'

Shaftesbury was vastly relieved. His mind was already stretched by worry about Accy who, serving on an overseas station and never writing home, had probably 'got into bad hands and practices'. Minny too was 'more harrassed', she told the steady Evelyn, 'then I dare own to your Papa, who is also very anxious and takes fire if he feels that others participate in those fears.'[1]

A month later Palmerston suffered several resignations and again turned to Shaftesbury. The newspapers wanted him, the Queen hinted that she would take it as a personal insult if he refused, his mother-in-law, busy Cabinet-making with her husband, wrote a hurried note telling him to come in, and Minny was imploring: 'I do *beseech* you,' she wrote from the country, 'not to refuse. Reflect how *much more* weight everything has, coming from a Cabinet Minister.'

'I was at my wit's end,' recalled Shaftesbury many years later. 'On one side was ranged wife, relations, friends, ambition, influence; on the other, my own objections, which seemed sometimes to weigh as nothing in comparison with the arguments brought against them. I could not satisfy myself that to accept office was a divine call; I *was* satisfied that God had called me to labour among the poor.' He longed for visible indication of God's will, like the Urim and Thummim of the Old Testament.

Minny had come home and was nagging at her Ashley for his good, as she saw it. Shaftesbury replied to Lady Palmerston: 'It is utterly impossible to express the grief and agony that I have undergone and am still undergoing. This affair has completely broken up my private and domestic peace.'

He still tried to refuse. Suddenly a note came from Lady Palmerston telling him to put on uniform and be at Buckingham Palace that afternoon to be sworn in. 'Pray do this, and I am *sure* you will not repent it.' Palmerston had sought

1. 'How many times have I, in my excitable spirit, said unjust and cruel things to her! What a placable spirit! What a power to forgive! and what a sublime power to forget!' Shaftesbury in his diary after Minny's death in 1872.

high and low for a substitute, in vain. He had decided to
force the issue, believing in his airy way that Shaftesbury's
conscientious objections would melt in the Cabinet room.

Unable to see clear guidance, Shaftesbury 'never felt so
helpless. I seemed to be hurried along without a will of my
own; without any power of resistance. I went and dressed,
and then, while I was waiting for the carriage I went down
on my knees and prayed for counsel, wisdom and understanding. Then, there was someone at the door; as I
thought, to say that the carriage was ready. Instead of that,
a note, hurriedly written in pencil, was put in my hands. It
was from Palmerston. "Don't go to the Palace."' Shaftesbury, middle-aged as he was, danced round the room for
joy. Lord Harrowby was willing to be his substitute.

*   *   *

Henceforth Shaftesbury had no difficulty in refusing offers
of Cabinet posts, such as the Home Secretaryship from
Lord Derby in 1866. And his fears of the 'disruption of
family ties' were not justified: the Palmerstons remained as
devoted to him as to Minny, and he to them.

Palmerston and Shaftesbury made unlikely close friends,
for 'Pam' was an arrant atheist who looked with tolerant
cynicism on Shaftesbury's deepest beliefs. But he was
lovable, human and shrewd, with an essential kindliness.
Shaftesbury was particularly grateful at this time because
Palmerston, when Home Secretary, had secured the passage of Shaftesbury's oft-opposed Bill to set up Reforma-
tories for Boys, which stopped the law treating convicted
small boys as if they were short adults and sending them to
ordinary prisons and even to the treadmill.

Moreover Palmerston was generous. He persuaded
Shaftesbury to accept the Garter. He had refused it from
Aberdeen because it was still primarily a political honour,
and because it required a high fee to the College of Arms.
Palmerston overcame Shaftesbury's scruples and, in the
most tactful and delicate way, paid the fees himself. A year
later, when Shaftesbury was passing sleepless nights be-

cause of intense financial pressures, Palmerston helped to set up Lionel, the fourth son, in business; 'a continuance of the constant goodness you have always shown to me,' wrote Minny in a glowing letter of thanks, adding, 'All I say is equally felt by Ashley, and how could it be otherwise?' Palmerston made Evelyn, the third son, his Private Secretary when he came down from Trinity College, Cambridge, thus forwarding Evelyn's political career and helping Shaftesbury financially.

The warmth of affection between the embodiment of the nineteenth-century conscience and the relic of eighteenth-century unbelief disclosed the breadth of Shaftesbury's sympathy. And it brought him a fresh and powerful opportunity for, in his own phrase, 'doing good'.

A Prime Minister had the sole patronage of every vacant bishopric, archbishopric and deanery. When Palmerston took office Shaftesbury bemoaned to Evelyn that 'Palmerston's ecclesiastical appointments will be detestable,' and said that the man could not tell the theological difference between Moses and Sydney Smith, the deistical wit, lately Canon of St. Paul's; his local vicar was the only clergyman he had spoken to, the religious feelings of the country were 'as strange to him as the interior of Japan', and he had only just heard of 'the grand heresy of the Puseyites and Tractarians'.

But Palmerston virtually turned over the whole Church patronage to his stepson-in-law, though sometimes he listened to others, or respected a request from the Queen. Shaftesbury thus became largely responsible, in the nine years of the two Premierships until Palmerston's death, for the appointment of no less than five archbishops and twenty bishops in England and Ireland. For the first time the despised Evangelicals received their due share, so that a bigoted Tractarian bishop declaimed about 'Palmerston's wicked appointments'. No man received preferment as a reward or bribe for political services, or on family grounds. 'I am a very lucky man,' said Palmerston to Shaftesbury, 'I have no sons, grandsons or nephews to stuff into the Church, and as far as all that is concerned I can do what I think right.' And he had no truck with arrogant clerics who despised or attacked Nonconformists.

Rather than dry dons, superannuated headmasters, or men with no claim but their lineage, Shaftesbury sought to make bishops of clergy who had worked hard in parishes, especially among the poor. Palmerston's first appointment on Shaftesbury's advice, to the see of Carlisle, was greeted with derision because Montague Villiers was little known in ecclesiastical high places and was brother of the Foreign Secretary, Lord Clarendon. But Villiers was vicar of St. George's, Bloomsbury, a parish of slums as well as middle class squares, and had led a team of curates, Scripture readers and London City Missionaries. He was a large man and a great preacher, especially to working class men. He was soon promoted from Carlisle to be Bishop of Durham, though no scholar, but died very soon.

The 'Shaftesbury Bishops' made their niche in church history and have been analysed and studied in depth. Shaftesbury exercised his unexpected responsibility with fairness. When he saw that Palmerston was firmly in power and the opportunity would not be fleeting, he was careful to balance his suggestions so that Palmerston could not be accused of favouritism. Shaftesbury looked primarily for men of God who would work hard for their people.

Few made great names, but several bishops and deans, whose memory lingered long in their dioceses or cathedral cities, were promoted to positions of influence which they might never have received in the then state of politics and the Church.

The story behind the appointment of the most famous of the Shaftesbury Bishops has never been told.

On a summer's day in 1856 Shaftesbury was in his library at Grosvenor Square when he learned that Lady Wake wished to see him. He guessed the reason. Lady Wake had been Charlotte Tait, the younger sister of the Lady Sitwell of those far off days of youthful gaiety in Derbyshire and Scotland. Their youngest brother, Archibald Campbell Tait, headmaster of Rugby, had been appointed Dean of Carlisle before he was forty, six years earlier; and all the world knew of the recent tragedy when the Taits had lost five of their seven small children from scarlet fever in the spring of 1856.

Shaftesbury welcomed her. 'Well I remember,' she wrote in an unpublished section of her Reminiscences, 'the feelings with which I entered his Library. We had not met since I was 18 and he was 20. He had of course risen to receive me, and there we stood for half a minute face to face each holding the other's hand, he I supposed like myself endeavouring to trace the original countenance in the present. It was difficult to recognise the face of the handsome sparkling boy I remembered so well, in the grave careworn countenance before me, but there was encouragement in its kind thoughtful expression.'

Lady Wake begged Shaftesbury to prevent her brother returning to his desolated home. 'Everyone tells me that Lord Palmerston is chiefly guided by your counsels in selecting who he ought to recommend to the Queen when there is a vacant Bishopric and I want to tell you what I myself personally know of my brother.' As she described Tait's pastoral and evangelistic work among all ages and classes in Carlisle, Shaftesbury seemed to listen coldly; but he became interested when she spoke of the children helping their father as he went among the poor, and how the scarlet fever had struck them one by one. She described 'as well as I could love the submission of all, as child after child had been given up into the Saviour's hands.'

Then she said: 'And now the nursery is empty, the house is utterly desolate. How can the Father and Mother return here? Oh Lord Shaftesbury, I am sure you will go to Lord Palmerston, and ask him to do that great kindness, which will give to the Church and the Country, the very best and most efficient of Bishops whenever he may have power to do so!'

Lady Wake saw that 'tears had fallen from the kind eyes that had been fixed in earnest attention; he had himself lately lost a son. No man on earth possessed a heart more full of feeling and he said. "I will indeed do what I can. I cannot promise to succeed, but I will try; I entirely believe all you say of your brother."'

Shaftesbury had already marked Tait as a coming man but, as he wrote to Lady Wake later: 'It was in no slight measure owing to your representation of what was in him that I urged his name upon the consideration of the Minister . . . I may say I believe that I stated your brother's qualifications to Lord Palmerston in the strongest manner adding that as he desired all sections of the Church of England to be represented, he could not do better than take on one who being neither Puseyite, High Church nor Evangelical was an admirable man, and full of zeal for the advancement of religion.'

Palmerston made Tait Bishop of London – a choice which was soon to help Shaftesbury's work among the poor in a very decided way.

16

A NEW USE FOR THEATRES

Exeter Hall had a narrow front on to the Strand, sand-
wiched between two halves of a hotel, and an auditorium
seating more than three thousand, pulled down in the next
century to make way for the Strand Palace Hotel. The
convenience of a hotel for supporters from the shires en-
sured Exeter Hall's popularity for the 'May Meetings' of
many religious societies until it had become almost synony-
mous with the Evangelical party. On the evening of Queen
Victoria's thirty-eighth birthday, 24 May 1857, it was the
scene of an unprecedented event which Shaftesbury described as 'a glorious triumph for religion and the Church of
England' – an evening service in a secular hall.

Two years previously he had secured the repeal of the
Act which, as the modern version of Charles II's Convent-
icle Act, had made illegal any religious service attended by
more than twenty people in a building not licensed for
worship. Though seldom invoked, the Act had put most of
the London City Mission's meetings outside the law, and
Shaftesbury knew of a northern landowner who began
cottage meetings for the numerous miners living at the
gates of his park, far from the parish church, yet had been
stopped by an information laid against him.

Shaftesbury had been strongly opposed. He was thinking only of the unreached masses, yet Tractarians joined
old High Churchmen in a phalanx of peers and prelates
who wanted no religious meeting without a parson. 'Derby
and his friends behind me while I spoke, insolent, interrup-

tive, discouraging. He seemed like a man who felt a deep
irritation at the movement and a hatred for the mover.
Faltered, at least to my own sensation, very greatly: was
awfully depressed, unhappy and diffident; nothing without in the House and nothing within my own heart to cheer
me.' He was disgusted that Derby would use his house or
barn for a cockfight but not in worship.

The Act which finally got passed was not as full an
emancipation as Shaftesbury had hoped but it made
possible the first evening service in Exeter Hall.

The new Bishop of London, Crauford Tait, had given his
warm approval, and the local incumbent agreed grudgingly. Posters were aimed particularly at those who did not
usually attend church or chapel, implying a warm welcome
for families from the poorest homes.

Evening services of the Church of England were rare in
1857, not so much because of cold in winter or the cost of
oil-lamps or candles, but because most pews were rented to
parishioners who would neither come of an evening nor
allow their pews to be used. But here on Queen Victoria's
birthday was a full house in the vast Exeter Hall, listening to
Villiers, the newly appointed 'Shaftesbury' Bishop of Carlisle, wearing full canonicals, as he preached the simple
Christian Gospel in the clear and popular way which had
made him famous as the parson of the squares and slums of
nearby Bloomsbury. Many working people came; but the
strength of the singing suggested that a part of the audience
was middle class.

The Exeter Hall evenings broke new ground. Sunday
after Sunday in that summer of the Indian Mutiny, when
the heat in London seemed of an almost Indian intensity,
especially indoors, hundreds had to be turned away. The
services stopped for September and were about to restart
when the vicar of the parish, whose Church of St. Michael's
was round the corner, revoked his consent and inhibited
the clergyman coming to officiate. The Bishop of London
regretfully advised compliance since the law was still un-
clear.

Nonconformists took over, with utmost tact. Shaftesbury

attended and saw by the clothes of the audience that many came from the working class; afterwards 'as I walked away I was almost overwhelmed with shame that the Church of England alone was excluded from holding such services.' He promptly introduced an Amending Bill to remove the power of an incumbent to inhibit another clergyman, except in small parishes. He was again opposed by the Bishop of Oxford, though he was son of the great Evangelical liberator of the slaves, William Wilberforce. A reasonable compromise was effected by the archbishop, but it did not reach the Statute Book. Meanwhile the Bishop of London, as a direct result of Exeter Hall, persuaded the Deans and Chapters of Westminster Abbey and St. Paul's to start winter evening services in 1858 which met with overwhelming popular success.

Exeter Hall services were resumed, free of trouble, but Shaftesbury and his friends wanted to reach the poorest. From January 1860 they astonished – and rather shocked – the polite world by hiring seven theatres every Sunday evening in the roughest parts, including Sadler's Wells, the famous Brittania in Hoxton, and the Old Vic in the New Cut, south of the river, a theatre noted for salacious entertainment in a road notorious for drunks, prostitutes, and crime.

Shaftesbury went to the Old Vic. Before going round to the stage he looked in at the house and found it crammed from the pit to the 'gods' with a smelly, excited crowd, whose clothes proved that they were London's poor. Men far outnumbered women. They stood or sat, packed tight, for there were as yet no fire regulations against overcrowding.

Shaftesbury found the manager and asked what kind of people they were. 'The man replied that there were 3,200 present he was certain, because he was expert at such calculations, from having to count the people in the theatre. And of that number 2,000 belonged to the class called "roughs" – the most violent, disorderly, and dangerous of all the men in that very quarter.

'This man lifted up his hands in amazement when he saw

how quiet was their demeanour. He had expected uproar
and even danger, and he frankly said he could not com-
prehend how those two thousand wild, unruly fellows
behaved themselves so well.'

Shaftesbury joined the clergy beyond the footlights. The
singing of the 'Old Hundredth' started a little uncertainly,
for this was before the days of Moody and Sankey hymns,
but they roared out the last verse. When the parson prayed,
the people showed reverence in any way which occurred to
them. Few knew the Lord's Prayer. Then Shaftesbury
prepared to read the lesson. Many recognised him and he
heard a murmur of approval but no interruption as he read,
very clearly and audibly, bringing out the sense.

He told the House of Lords afterwards: 'From the beginning to the end of the service no assembly could have been
more orderly, more attentive, more apparently devout, and
more anxious to catch every word that fell from the
preacher's lips. On one of the occasions, so solemn and
touching was the discourse of the preacher, and so moved
were many even of the wildest and roughest present, that
when, after the "Benediction," they rose to leave the building, they went so quietly and solemnly that you could
hardly hear the sound of a footfall.

'Surely no one can deny that a deep and solemn impression is made on the minds of those people: it is found that
many come to the services week after week; and can it be
doubted that we are by degrees spreading a leaven
throughout the whole population?'

On one Sunday in February 1860 it was reckoned that a
total of more than eighteen thousand attended the theatre
services, and none of the local churches, Anglican or Nonconformist, reported any loss of numbers. 'My Lords,' said
Shaftesbury to the House of Lords when an Irish peer
attacked the services, 'you must perceive the rising struggle
to preach the Gospel among this mighty mass of human
beings . . .' Two years later, he encouraged the Church
Pastoral Aid Society's annual meeting to see the theatre
services as evidence of the 'mighty change' in the working
classes since the early eighteen-thirties: 'Look at the great

things which have been done . . . I say that thirty years ago the mention of such a thing would have brought dismay to the heart. We have not only mentioned it, but we have done it.

'Think of the rough, uncouth, wild, and half-savage creatures, male and female, who came there, – persons of such strange aspect and appearance that many who saw them for the first time, pressing forward on the front benches, could hardly imagine where they came from. Well, there they sat, mute and motionless, with open eyes, drinking in, with grateful hearts, the pure and simple Gospel which was addressed to them.' And he went on to describe Dean Close (Dean of Carlisle) on the stage of the Old Vic, 'talking with his simplicity of speech and fervency of heart to the people who were assembled, about Christ and his great salvation'.

The theatre services became a feature of mid-Victorian London, reaching thousands hitherto untouched and bringing them into the life of church or chapel.

17

LORD OF THE MANOR

During the London season of 1860 the Shaftesburys' four daughters, ranging in age from twenty-three to thirteen, went twice a week with their governess to help and read to the young cripples in the orthopaedic hospital, a blessing 'to the teachers and the taught. Never have I felt more joy,' wrote Shaftesbury, 'than to see that the more wretched the object, the more degraded and helpless the sufferer, the greater the sympathy of my children, and the greater their devotion.' Even Accy made a good speech at the Ragged School Union's annual meeting.

But Accy grieved his parents frequently, though affection was never broken on either side. Once he was arrested for debt and had to be bailed out and the debt paid, a loss that Shaftesbury could ill afford. In 1857 Lord Ashley, as Accy was now styled, stood for Parliament at Hull, his father hoping that a seat in the House would steady him. Evelyn was sent to help. ('I am very glad to hear old Edy is coming as it will be somebody to sit with and talk to in the evening.') Evelyn, acting the older brother although five years younger, sent their father encouraging reports: 'He is the only Conservative candidate and *your name* works wonders. Upon my life he will be bound to act up to the name he has inherited if he is returned.' Accy won the seat but made no mark in Parliament. Soon afterwards he married Lady Harriet Chichester, daughter of the Marquess of Donegal, who was generally in debt. Shaftesbury knew little about her, and nothing bad, but soon found her decidedly worldly and domineering. For some years she kept herself and the grandchildren away from her father-in-law as much as she could, to his sorrow.

The Ashley family now comprised the four daughters and four surviving sons, the gentle, epileptic Maurice having died in 1855, aged twenty, at Lausanne. Mary, the second daughter, was to die of 'consumption' (tuberculosis) in 1861 after a distressing illness: her death was one of the few times when Shaftesbury's faith in the love and wisdom of God was shaken: he had prayed, when all hope had gone, that hers should be a happy death in broad daylight, but she died in great pain during the night.

When the eighteen-sixties began, Accy was nearly thirty, Evelyn, at twenty-four, was working with Palmerston, Lionel (Vava) was a very young man in business, and Cecil was coming up to eleven years of age: 'Buckingham Palace, 24th February 1860. Major Elphinstone presents his compliments to the Countess of Shaftesbury, and has been requested by H.R.H. Prince Arthur, to ascertain whether her son Cecil Ashley is in town, and if so, whether he would be permitted to play with H.R.H. this afternoon between 3 and 5 p.m. in Buckingham Palace Gardens.'

*   *   *

When Parliament was in session the Shaftesburys were usually at Grosvenor Square. Shaftesbury would have preferred spending much of the Recess (which continued throughout autumn) at St. Giles's, except for their annual seaside holiday in Scotland; but Minny liked Ems or another Continental watering place, and thus he had less time at The Saint than he wished.

He was slowly getting house and estate in order but finding both to be a drain on his straitened finances. The north wing of the house was falling down when he inherited. After he had put the worst cottages in order and built schools (selling surplus plate to finance them) he began on the house, employing the well known partnership of Philip Hardwick, architect of Euston Station and several famous buildings, and his son Philip, who probably did the work. Hardwick had extravagant ideas. Shaftesbury, like Palmerston who added the 'Bachelor' wing to Georgian Broadlands, wanted plenty of room for family, guests and servants but Hardwick designed the new north wing unnecessarily large and added fancy towers. To give local employment Shaftesbury had the bricks made on the estate. He rejoiced to see a whole army of labourers and gave them a day off for a cricket match. But Hardwick never came down from London to superintend Holland the builder. The construction was shoddy and caused endless later expense. Shaftesbury therefore refused to pay Hardwick more than a token fee of £200.

Shaftesbury added a new portico to the house. And here, in 1859, with Matthew Noble the sculptor present, he placed the fine bust of himself which the factory workers of the north had presented to Minny in gratitude for the Factory Acts. Thousands had each given one penny towards it, and the Shaftesburys had been much moved at the presentation in Manchester.

That same year fourteen hundred teachers of the Ragged Schools in London clubbed together to present a small painting, the 'Shoe Black's Dinner', which soon became well known from prints. He hung it at Grosvenor Square, and would lovingly show the finely bound accompanying volume which contained an inscribed address and the signatures of all the donors. Shaftesbury would point out their variety of callings. Some lawyers, clergy and bankers but mostly: *William H. White, Brush maker; John Kitchener, Warehouseman; Mary Pecord, Cook; Sarah Halford, Stay Maker* . . . Clerks and gardeners, pawnbrokers and cow-keepers, hosiers, hatters and grocers, one hundred and twenty trades in all, an extraordinary range of Christians working together. 'I would rather be President of the Ragged School Union than have the command of armies or wield the destinies of empires,' Shaftesbury had said in reply to the address.

Down at The Saint, as he walked out of the new portico, with its bust, and down the drive to the village, Shaftesbury could take some satisfaction from the signs that Wimborne St. Giles was on its way to becoming a model estate in days when the condition of the rural population lay almost entirely in the hands of the landowners. He placed each cottage well back from the road, believing that cottagers soon turned any area at the back into a mess but would beautify the front as a garden.

He kept a sharp eye on their morals. Back in 1854 he had written to the aged rector, Prebendary Robert Moore: 'The population of the parish seems to be in a very low moral state. The young men are especially coarse, brutal and mischievous by your representations, and I find them far worse than you describe them to me.' He had to prod the easy-going Moore, 'as it is very undesirable that I and the minister of the parish should be in open collision'. By 1860 Moore had been the incumbent for thirty-seven years and his health was failing, yet it would be another five years before he died in office, at the age of eighty-one, and Shaftesbury, as patron, could present a man after his own heart.

Shaftesbury could be stern, as when Frampton the parish clerk got Jane Hart with child and denied it 'before Mr. Moore and "as in the presence of Almighty God."'; or when Gould the shoemaker allowed his cottage to fall into 'a very filthy, disgraceful and even dangerous state. I cannot,' wrote the earl, 'in reference to myself and to the villagers, allow this to continue.' He always sought to balance justice with kindness. He worked hard for the welfare of the villagers, as when he organised milk supplies against the wishes of the farmers. He undertook drainage to improve the land and to provide employment; unfortunately he did not realise that the drainage scheme offered his agent, Robert Waters, further opportunities to embezzle.

And always, in the flow of estate correspondence, came the occasional touching or amusing letter: 'My Lord, please to permit me to draw your attention to the bite of your dog,' wrote an old soldier, who had been hawking pins round the farms. 'On opening the gate your sheepdog flew at my hand and tore 2 of my fingers with his teeth.' The man wanted help as the damage had kept him off the roads. He wrote almost immediately, and yet again: 'My Lord, I again umblely request you to pay attention to my umble request.

'I have retten you 2 letters stateing whare the dog bit me . . . have received no reply it is deep regret I have to state my Lord, to think that a poor man in my umble cercom-stances reduced throuth the bite of your sheep dog to want a Bit of Brad and moust umblely ask you to send me a few shilling to inable me to come to show you my fingers and pouint out the cottage and the woman that draped my hand with some rags . . .'

The estate records do not show what happened, but Shaftesbury would certainly have done right by the old soldier.

*   *   *

The estate increasingly became a drain on Shaftesbury's resources, until all the county except himself knew he was being embezzled by Waters, the agent since 1845, a racing man who lived above his station. At last Lord Palmerston, in his tactful kindly way, opened his stepson-in-law's eyes to the robbery under his nose.

At Palmerston's suggestion Shaftesbury sent his London solicitors to investigate. Waters had been up to mischief for years and had destroyed incriminating evidence. Evelyn, now called to the Bar and newly back from an adventurous visit to Poland during the insurrection of 1863, offered to be at The Saint when his father came down to face Waters, 'if Papa the least wished it. But he may prefer,' Evelyn wrote to his mother, 'my being out of the way – but oh! the revelations they make one's blood alternately boil and creep.' He added a postscript: 'I am very fearful of Papa considering me interfering but he must know that my motives are the best.'

Waters was dismissed. He then sued Shaftesbury on flimsiest grounds, and good money went after bad.

Shaftesbury lost at least £50,000 through Waters' pecu-
lations and litigation, and would have been hard pressed
had not four or five rich Evangelical men of business
clubbed together to persuade him to accept a substantial
interest-free loan.

The Saint survived. 'Good-bye, my dear Lord,' said
Disraeli in his flowery way, after being brought over by a
neighbour, 'you have given me the privilege of seeing one
of the most impressive of all spectacles – a great English
nobleman living in patriarchal state in his own hereditary
halls.' Shaftesbury was much amused. (He had a low
opinion of D'Israeli, as he always spelt him. At the time of
the Congress of Berlin he described him to a friend as
'perhaps the most unwise, untrustworthy and pernicious
minister that ever held office in the realm of England.')

It was the poor, rather than his great neighbours, that
Shaftesbury loved to see at The Saint. In the galleried great
hall, which in earlier centuries had been a courtyard but
was now roofed with glass, on every Sunday night he held
a 'service of song', with family, visitors, servants and
nearby cottagers gathered together for hymn-singing, the
dogs carefully excluded. One of the household played the
organ, hymn after hymn was sung, and the earl would
close with a reading from the Bible and a brief prayer. Each
morning he led family prayers, which ended with a solemn
handshake for the elderly housekeeper and the rushed
entrance of the dogs.

Shaftesbury was adored by his people. On winter evenings, over wood fires in the cottages, they would tell of his
deeds; of the day, for instance, when he was driving over to
take the salute at a review during manoeuvres, and passed
an old woman hobbling along. He put her in the carriage.
When the thousand troops presented arms to the Lord
Lieutenant of Dorset they saw him sitting in full uniform on
the box beside the coachman, and the embarrassed old
villager in the place of honour behind.

He often visited the cottages. Once, coming up the path
to see a small girl reported sick, he heard her mother
shout, 'Hie thee to bed, Jane, get big Boible out, 'ere's Lord

Shaasbree a-coming.' When he entered, he found Jane in bed with a pious expression, and the Bible open on the bedclothes, upside down at the Book of Amos.

18

CONTENDING FOR ENGLAND'S FUTURE

As Shaftesbury rode through the twisting Dorset lanes to the market town of Blandford, or sat in the railway which idled through the countryside, he often noticed children at work in the fields, generally with their parents. The sight reminded him of an iniquity in East Anglia and some of the counties of the southern Midlands: the use of agricultural gangs. The law still allowed ruthless men to work small children beyond the point of exhaustion for a pittance; their backs bent as they hoed or weeded, with hours so long that no time or energy was left for schooling or fun.

When he had first learned about the gangs he could do nothing. 'The agricultural part of the question,' he said afterwards, 'was reserved to the last; first, because it presented the greatest difficulties; and secondly, because it required all the sympathy and experience to be derived from the proof of success, furnished by the factories, to obtain for it a favourable reception.' Not until he was sixty-four, in 1865, was he able to plead the cause of children in the fields to a House of Lords composed almost exclusively of landowners. Two years later, after prolonged enquiry and a speech as impassioned as his famous appeal for children in the mines over twenty years earlier, he obtained a Bill which somewhat limited the agricultural labour of the young; though it was nine years more before a Tory Government, in the Education Act which sent every child to school, outlawed the employment in the fields of any child under ten.

Another loophole in the Children's Employment Acts came to his notice: the hard labour of small children in the brickfields. A Methodist local preacher in Coalville, Leicestershire, George Smith, had suffered as a child in his uncle's brickfield. He had long determined to crusade against the practice but no opportunity came until 1863. Aided by an inspector of factories he began to agitate. He sent one of his pamphlets to Shaftesbury, who replied: 'This state of things is simply wicked, and the continuance of it without excuse.'

Shaftesbury went down to a brickfield. 'I saw at a distance what appeared like eight or ten pillars of clay.' As he approached he was astonished to find that these were children, filthy with clay, who ran screaming at the sight of a gentleman. He followed them to their work. 'I saw little children, three parts naked, tottering under the weight of wet clay – some of it on their heads and some on their shoulders – and little girls with huge masses of wet, cold and dripping clay pressed on their abdomens.' He watched as they carried the loads to the kilns, where they 'had to enter places where the heat was so fierce that I was not myself able to remain more than two or three minutes'.

In 1871 A. J. Mundella, a Liberal Member for Sheffield, brought in a Bill, while Shaftesbury moved an Address in the Lords, exclaiming that what he had seen in the brickfields 'was a disgrace to the country and ought not for a moment to be allowed to continue'. He carried the Address, but Mundella had a stiff fight in the House of Commons before child employment ended.

Nearly a quarter of a century had passed since the Factory Act of 1847 and still Shaftesbury had to fight for the freedom of children where the law allowed tyranny. His attempts to free the climbing boys had failed again and again. When his Sweeps Bill of 1854 was thrown out he had been puzzled why a good cause should not be blessed: 'Again I must bow to this mysterious Providence that leaves these outcasts to their horrible destiny, and nullifies all our efforts to rescue them in soul and body . . . I must persevere, for however

dark the view, however painful and revolting the labour, I
see no Scripture reason for desisting; and the issue of every
toil is in the hands of the Almighty.'

The hero of Charles Kingsley's *The Water Babies* was a
climbing boy, but though the public of 1863 delighted in the
fairy tale it took for granted the existence of the 'helpless
and miserable race' as Shaftesbury described them. It was
at this time, on hearing of a fashionable woman's remark,
'A chimney sweep, indeed, wanting education! What
next?' that Shaftesbury shocked the Lords by exclaiming
that a woman like that 'would cut up a child for dog's meat
or for making manure'. Not until 1875 did the death of a
fourteen-year-old George Brewster, after swallowing soot
in a flue at Cambridge and being beaten by his master,
rouse public opinion enough to make Parliament pass the
Shaftesbury Act which abolished the practice for ever.

Long after Shaftesbury was dead a speaker at a public
meeting was astonished at exceptional applause produced
by a casual mention of the name. He asked what they knew
of him. A man arose and shouted, 'Know of him? Why, I'm
a chimbley sweep, and what did he do for me? Didn't he
pass the Bill? When I was a little 'un I had to go up
chimbleys, and many a time I've come down with bleedin'
feet and knees and a'most choking. And he passed the Bill
and saved us from all that. That's what I know, Sir, of Lord
Shaftesbury.'

*   *   *

While Shaftesbury fought to improve social conditions by
legislation he was also 'contending for the Faith', without
which all social improvement must be barren and fleeting.

Contention, rather than polemic (and never personal
abuse, though he could speak strongly and directly) was
the breath of life to him: if he saw a wrong he leaped to
correct it, whether a social wrong or a heresy; and therefore
an enormous body of his written or reported words may be
consulted for his views.

In his earlier years as a public figure he rejoiced that vital

Christianity gained an ever increasing hold on the nation, so that the nineteenth century was sweeping away the infidelities of the eighteenth, and putting right, though all too slowly, the social injustices which it had bred. As he grew older he became more and more concerned that Christian England was being undermined. He deplored the views of the Tractarians (or Puseyites, the term he preferred) as promoting heresy: he contended that they exalted the sacraments into a place not given them by the teaching of Christ or his apostles; that they claimed for the Church a higher authority than the Bible, and taught that a priest had a power not granted to a layman, who must come to God through priestly ministrations. When Ritualism became an issue he fought it, in Parliament and out, because vestments and stoles were the acknowledged symbols of a priest who stood between God and the people: not for another hundred years would the Church of England officially declare the wearing of a stole to have no doctrinal significance.

Even more dangerous was the rising tide of Rationalism. Shaftesbury, as an amateur scientist, was not dismayed by the strident claims of Huxley, Tyndall and some other scientists that the discoveries and conclusions of Darwin and themselves had disproved the Bible and rendered God superfluous to mankind, if He existed (Huxley had not yet coined his term *agnostic*). Mid-Victorian scientists had made such leaps forward that some spoke and wrote as if they had explained the origin and function of all matters in the universe.

To Shaftesbury, true science and true religion were allies: and he gladly became president of a new learned society, the Victoria Institute, at which eminent men discussed the issues. 'Were I wealthy and powerful,' he wrote in his diary four years after the famous 'Apes or Angels' debate at Oxford, when Huxley worsted Bishop Wilberforce, 'I would give enormous sums for the advancement of science. I would make no conditions . . .' He was certain that science would vindicate the Bible.

He reacted sharply, however, to theological liberalism

and the trends of higher criticism, or 'Neology' as he called it, using the term invented in the early nineteenth century by opponents of the southern German school of Biblical critics. In 1860, with many leading churchmen of the day, though in a more forthright manner than most, he rejected the views put forth by seven learned men in the celebrated *Essays and Reviews*; their watered down Christianity could never have helped a Ragged School child. He recommended promotion for the learned men who answered them.

One pleasing result of the long drawn out controversy was a reconciliation with Pusey, his cousin and Oxford contemporary. When Pusey wrote to the Evangelical newspaper, the *Record*, calling upon all Christians to forego minor differences and unite against the great doctrinal errors of the day, Shaftesbury at once sent him a warm letter: 'We have to struggle . . . for the very Atonement itself, for the sole hope of fallen men, the vicarious sacrifice of the Cross,' wrote Shaftesbury. 'For God's sake let all who love our blessed Lord, and His perfect Word, be of one heart, one mind, one action on this great issue, and show that, despite our wanderings, our doubts, our contentions, we may yet be one in Him.'

Pusey replied equally warmly and lovingly. When Pusey died, eighteen years later, Shaftesbury noted: 'Intensely and fearfully as I differed from him in matters of unspeakable importance, I could not but love the man.'

In 1865 Shaftesbury received a copy of a new, anonymous book, *Ecce Homo*. It used the Gospels to present a Christ who was a good man, a profound teacher and a worker of miracles but not the Son of God. When Shaftesbury was preparing his speech for the next Church Pastoral Aid annual meeting he resolved to denounce it as 'a most pestilential book'. During the speech, speaking rapidly and warmly as he generally did, and freed from his rule against uttering personalities by the book's anonymity, he let himself go, and was astonished to read next morning that in 'the heat of declamation' he had called *Ecce Homo* 'the most pestilential book ever to be vomited from the jaws of hell!'

This impromptu ('justified, yet injudicious') brought wrath on his head and such publicity for the book that the author, revealed as J. R. Seeley (son of an old acquaintance), gleefully claimed that Shaftesbury had gained him 10,000 copies and put £1,000 in his pocket.

Shaftesbury did not seek contention; he responded to the need as he saw it. The controversies of the age depressed him. His high hopes for England, and through England the world, were slowly dying as he watched men arguing when they should have been evangelising.

Unlike William Wilberforce he was not an optimist by nature. One springtime in the early seventies he and Minny had taken Constance, ill with tuberculosis, to Italy and the south of France. They reached Mentone, and here his friend Charles Haddon Spurgeon, the young and famous Baptist preacher, was also staying to recover from overwork. Spurgeon wrote to his wife: 'Just before dinner, who should go by but the Earl of Shaftesbury, with whom I had half-an-hour's conversation. He was very low in spirit, and talked as if all things in the world were going wrong; but I reminded him that our God is yet alive, and that dark days were only the signs of better times coming. He is a real nobleman, and man of God.'

Shaftesbury had a reputation in the House of Lords and in the counsels of the Church as a Prophet Jeremiah. He spoke often of the good that might be done, but could not forbear to warn of the dangers ahead. Shaftesbury saw more clearly than most that the glories of the nineteenth century would wither away unless men changed their course. His one hope lay, as always, in the Second Coming of Christ.

*　　*　　*

However much time Shaftesbury might spend on controversy his great delight was to spread the Gospel of Christ. He loved to go about London, not only to ease the social needs of the poor but to reach their souls.

He would walk along, his tall frame easily recognised, to

encourage the work of his many societies. He would visit one of the new Cabmen's Shelters, which served good food and non-intoxicating drink, thus keeping waiting cabmen from the public houses; or he would inspect the drinking fountains and horse-troughs which another of his societies had erected for the comfort of man and beast; or look in at the Newsboys' Refuge: 'What a rough unwashed uncombed lot!' He would always stop for a chat and perhaps a laugh with a shoeblack boy.

Once, after a walk through the slums, he discovered that Maria Milles's gold watch, his most precious possession, had been picked from his pocket. He appealed to his friends of the underworld. A few nights later a large, squirming canvas bag was deposited on his doorstep. Shaftesbury and his butler opened it. A small urchin was inside along with the watch and a note from other vagabonds pinned to the boy's rags demanding that the thief should get what he deserved. Shaftesbury placed him in a school.

One of his favourite and frequent calls was to the George Yard Mission in Whitechapel founded by George Holland, a man of some substance who devoted his life to the poor and had built up, from a Ragged School, an extensive work of relief, education and spiritual succour. Shaftesbury admired and trusted him: 'In all my experience I have found very few to come near him; and none to surpass him. His zeal and sympathy are so strong that they cannot be wearied.' His work lay 'in the midst of filth, cold, and hunger and nakedness . . . what would give most people a nausea seems to give him an appetite.'

Shaftesbury presented two magic lanterns to the George Yard Mission and sometimes would sit with the East Enders as Holland or another used them. And sometimes he would use them himself. One evening four or five hundred of all ages were at a magic lantern lecture he was giving on the Cross, and many had been turned away: 'The interest in the pictures was intense,' he recalled, 'and I shall never forget their earnest, excited faces as the scenes of the sacred drama passed before them. The last picture represented our Lord standing beside a closed door, and the text at the foot of the picture was, "Behold, I stand at the door and knock." The effect was startling – it seemed to bring the story home to every heart, and when I said, "What you see there is going on at the door of every house in Whitechapel," they were moved to tears. When I told them that if they would throw open the door He would "come in and sup with them", there was something so cosy and comfortable in the idea of it that they came pouring round me and thanking me.'

19

SEA LEGS AND COSTERS

On a cold wet night in February 1866 Shaftesbury directed his coachman to drive him to the Boys' Refuge in Great Queen Street between Drury Lane and Lincoln's Inn, where some of the worst slums jostled with lawyer's chambers. The way was familiar: the coachman had often taken his lordship in the year or two since the Refuge had been founded by William Williams, a solicitor's clerk and a Ragged School worker.

As they drove up, an extraordinary sight met the coachman's eyes – under the gaslight of the street he saw scores of dirty small boys, mostly barefoot and in rags but each clutching a ticket. They were entering the Refuge chattering loudly, but they made way for the elderly Lord Shaftesbury: some recognised his gaunt face as he smiled gravely, yet with a twinkle in his eye. William Williams, who had been a cripple since boyhood, limped up to greet him, and told him that some four hundred invitations to his Lordship's dinner had been offered through City missionaries, Ragged Schools and casual wards. Some boys, Williams had heard, refused because they thought it a trap, others were afraid that 'we will get lots of jaw and nothing to eat.' About one hundred and fifty had given in their names, received tickets and arrived.

Shaftesbury watched the boys as they noisily took their places at tables piled high with bread and butter, with enticing knives, forks and spoons to show that much more was coming. He knew that many were orphans or had only one parent, often 'of a most dissolute character. They had been accustomed,' he said afterwards, 'to sleep in dry arches, in old iron rollers, or any place in which they could nestle; and many of the boys were clear in their assertions that for years they had never been inside a bed.' And most of them had not received the slightest education, though a few had occasionally attended a Ragged School.

After nearly a quarter of a century of Ragged Schools and emigration schemes Shaftesbury grieved that the problem of destitute children was still unresolved. For fifteen years or more he had dreamed of a possible answer but the hazards had seemed too great; now at last he had determined to put it to the proof, and the first step was to invite these street arabs to dinner.

Great plates of roast beef passed down the tables to roars of delight and popping of eyes. Some of the boys hardly knew how to use a fork, and wolfed down the meat and potatoes and scooped up the gravy with their bread. Silence had descended as they concentrated on this meal of a lifetime. Behind the tables, watching the willing assistants as they served and the ragged boys as they ate, were a few journalists and some well dressed ladies and gentlemen. Shaftesbury had invited them to witness the feast, with an eye to their pocket books for the scheme he had in mind. Some were near to tears as they saw what stark poverty could mean to a child.

Plum pudding followed, as much as any boy could eat; then coffee. When all had eaten, and fortunately none of the more hungry had been sick, the superintendent called out that they were all to move downstairs to another room. With a grinding of chairs and bursts of chat and merriment they all rushed, so well fed that none of them pinched knife or spoon, and scrambled for seats on the benches. As Lord Shaftesbury and Williams mounted the platform the boys cheered them to the echo.

Williams put up his hand and at last obtained quiet, except for an occasional belch. 'His lordship wishes to address you,' he said.

Shaftesbury looked around at these boys, all under sixteen and many very young. All pathetically ragged and most of them smelly.

'I am going to ask you some questions, boys,' he began, 'and I want you to tell the truth. We only want your good; you need not conceal anything.

'Let all those boys who have ever been in prison hold up their hands.' About twenty or thirty hands shot up.

'Let those who have been in prison twice hold up their hands.' About ten.

'How many in prison three times?' Five.

'Is it the case that the greater part of you boys are running about town all day, and sleeping where you can at night?' He heard a general murmur of assent.

'How do you get your livelihood?' Answers came from all over the hall. 'Holding horses' – 'Begging' – 'Cleaning boots.'

'Would you like to get out of your present line of life and into one of honest industry?' asked Shaftesbury. A loud and generally 'Yes' was the answer.

'Supposing that there were, in the Thames, a big ship, large enough to contain a thousand boys. Would you like to be placed on board to be taught trades, or trained for the navy and merchant service?'

Shouts of 'Yes' and a forest of hands.

'Do you think that another 200 boys out of the streets would say the same?' Again a murmur of assent.

Shaftesbury sent them away with words of encouragement, though only too aware that some of them might spend the cold wet night under tarpaulins on rooftops or under bridges.

Next day he spoke to the First Lord of the Admiralty, the Duke of Somerset who as Lord Seymour had been so obstructive in the matter of a pure water supply sixteen years before. Shaftesbury and Somerset had been invested as Knights of the Garter on the same day in 1862. The Duke and his Lords of the Admiralty wanted men for the Royal Navy and the merchant marine and they had too many ships in peacetime. They looked around for a vessel, encouraged by *The Times*. Meanwhile the Committee of the

Refuges, an offshoot of the Ragged School Union, laid plans to buy or lease one or more houses near London as training homes for boys who did not want to go to sea, and for girls.

The boys ran ahead of the scheme. The very next day after the feast some fifty or sixty, singly and in groups, came to the door of Williams' Boys Refuge and asked to be taken in to be taught a trade. Williams did not hesitate.

Shaftesbury soon heard warm reports. They were working well, did not quarrel or even swear. One day, on the spur of the moment, he told the coachman to drive him to Great Queen Street. He arrived to find Williams in bed with pleurisy. 'The whole of that large number of boys were in consequence left without any control, excepting the old cobbler, whose post was in a remote corner; and yet I found them in the greatest order, carrying on their work, going regularly to the schoolmaster with their day's task, and steady in the course of all their operations. Not a single disturbance, not a single act of rebellion, not a single act of misconduct had to be reported, and so well pleased was I with the conduct of the boys that I called them together, and said to them, "Boys, this is the best thing I have ever seen. We put you here, we gave you a good chance, and now we see that we can trust you;" then a general shout of "Yes, you can."'

Shaftesbury told this to the meeting which he convened in April 1866 to set up a trust to run the promised training ship and the homes. He told it 'to prove to you that it is not true, as is sometimes urged, that such lads are utterly incorrigible, and must be left to the ordinary operations of the law.' As he put it on another occasion, 'If you take out of the streets of London all these homeless, most friendless and most destitute lads, polish them gently, and apply the hand of skill and affection, they will turn out diamonds.'

The Lords of the Admiralty produced a fifty-gun sail-rigged frigate, *Chichester*, which had never been to sea. The idea caught the imagination of a public brought up on romantic notions of 'wooden walls' and Jack Tars, and they

subscribed freely to fit her out. On 6 November Shaftesbury
took the train to Poplar to see her being adapted as a school.
A few days before Christmas 1866 he returned to inaugu-
rate the ship with a well scrubbed company of eager boys,
in the presence of a large gathering which included sea
captains and shipowners. In a rousing speech he looked to
the day when two hundred boys a year would go to sea
from the *Chichester* and her sister ships, 'fully capable of
undertaking their duties and gathered from the wandering
lads of London'. He called it a scandal that the merchant
marine in recent years had been largely crewed by foreigners.

He urged better ships (for this was before the Plimsoll
reforms) and a good endowment for the scheme now being
launched. He painted the possibilities in glowing terms: 'I
can foresee the time, notwithstanding the great and present
difficulties, notwithstanding the vast multitudes that
throng around, and which must make us stand aghast to
view the amount of misery and crime that now abounds in
the midst of us; I can foresee the time when by the applica-
tion of zeal and the multiplication of institutions like this,
the population of England, instead of becoming a curse
would become a blessing. And above all, they would give a
sound, religious, Christian education to these boys, who
would be sent to all ports and harbours of the world, by
their good conduct removing whatever was now a blot
upon the honour and name of the country.

'Instead of bringing drunkenness, disorder, and disgrace
into our navy, our vessels would in future be manned by
intelligent, well-conducted, and good-disciplined men –
the character of the English sailor would no longer be
such that it should be said of him that he was of all those
afloat by far the most profligate. The boys educated on
board this ship would show quite the reverse of this; they
would show to the whole earth what the British nation
really was, and what it would continue to be; and they
would enable us to repeat with certainty, with joy, and
with assurance, the words of the hymn that has just been
heard:

"Through every land, by every tongue,
Let the Redeemer's name be sung."'

The *Chichester* was followed after a few years by its more famous sister ship, *Arethusa*. On land, Shaftesbury Homes (as they were later named) and Schools were opened at two places near London to train destitute and homeless boys for emigration to the colonies, and two homes for girls. The dinner on the February night had begun a work which continued, adapting to changing conditions and generations, and serving as a beacon to later schemes: Thomas Barnardo came to London in the year of the feast and began his Homes a few years afterwards. Shaftesbury helped him, though at times doubting his judgment. Eventually Barnardo allowed the public, with its short memory, to believe that it was he who had opened Shaftesbury's eyes to the existence of homeless boys.

*   *   *

During the autumn of 1868 Shaftesbury heard about a new and most successful social and religious enterprise in a part of the City of London where slums and poverty were notorious. A young clerk in the General Post Office was having a marked influence on costermongers, the closeknit hereditary fraternity of general street traders.

Shaftesbury had already accepted the presidency or chairmanship of numerous missions and movements. Each meant more inspecting, more letters, more speeches and committees, more arbitrating and advising. The patronage of the Earl of Shaftesbury was widely sought and seldom refused if the cause was sound and worthy.

The young clerk, William Orsman, had not dared to seek it; but an encouraging letter arrived in the earl's own hand, offering to be president of this new Golden Lane mission. When Shaftesbury returned to London he paid the costers a visit.

Costermongers bought fruit (centuries earlier they had been called costard-mongers after a variety of apple), fish and vegetables at markets and sold them in the back streets from barrows drawn by donkeys. Costers were almost a race of their own, like gypsies, having passed trade secrets and colourful customs from generation to generation. They dressed spectacularly when they could, acknowledged their own 'pearly kings and queens' and had coined many of the slang words and phrases which cockneys used. Rough and jolly, uneducated, independent, never entering a church except to be married, they had their own codes of honour. Life was hard, especially since the new railway yards had engulfed their old haunts so that costers congregated in tenements, often two or more families and their donkeys in one room, with the produce stuffed under the beds.

A coster, as one of them remarked to young Orsman, was 'a cove wot works werry 'ard for a werry poor livin', and is always a-being interferred with, and blowed up, and moved hon, and fined, and sent to quod by the beaks and bobbies.' Shaftesbury took to them at once, and to William Orsman, a cheerful optimist whom no difficulties could deflate. Born in Cambridge he had volunteered as a youth to the civil commissariat in the Crimean War; his work attracted the favourable notice of Florence Nightingale. After the war, while in the lower ranks of the Post Office, he found his soul as an ardent Christian believer through the preaching of Spurgeon, who had begun his ministry in Cambridge before becoming at an early age the most famous Nonconformist preacher of the day. Orsman found his vocation when he happened to help some costers of Golden Lane in difficulties with the City authorities. The costers trusted him, and responded to his happy ways and unashamed faith. By the time Shaftesbury came the Golden Lane mission was already disclosing new horizons to the costers and improving their conditions.

Orsman had organised a Barrow and Donkey Club to help costers save to buy their own, instead of hiring at ruinous rates. Shaftesbury enrolled at once, subscribed for a donkey and barrow, had it decorated with his arms, and lent to a succession of deserving costers who were saving for their own. With his deep love of animals, and as vice-president of the R.S.P.C.A., he began donkey inspections, and by prizes and exhortation taught the men to treat the animals kindly. He interceded for them when the authorities were difficult.

In return, the costers enrolled him as one of themselves. It gave him special pleasure to be a coster. Once, when they asked him where they should write when they needed his help, he said, 'Address your letter to Grosvenor Square and it will probably reach me. But if after my name put "K.G. and Coster", there will be no doubt that I shall get it!' He would often say that after K.G. he mentally added A.C. – 'And Coster'.

He visited their homes, listened to their problems, and loved spending social evenings with his 'brethren'. His simple talks could hold them, though his being a peer must have helped their attention. One May morning he wrote in his diary: 'A wonderful meeting in Golden Lane last night. A spectacle to gladden angels – comfort, decency, education, in the midst of filth, destitution, vice and misery.' He wrote of Orsman's dedication and self sacrifice: 'It was enough to humble me.' And he added, intending in that aristocratic age no hint of condescension: 'Few things are more marvellous than to see what can be done by one man, however socially inferior, if he have but the love of Christ in his heart, and the Grace of our Lord to lead him on.' (Orsman not only built up the Mission in his spare time but rose in his profession, ending as Superintendent of Mails at the General Post Office and a London county councillor.)

Some seven years after Shaftesbury had become a coster he found himself chairing a most unusual meeting. A thousand costermongers, including the pearly king and queen, had gathered in the hall of the Golden Lane Mission following a donkey show, at which some of the donkeys wore placards: *Does not work on Sundays* – a weekly rest unknown to them a few years before.

After Shaftesbury had opened the meeting with a prayer, a Bible reading and his chairman's speech, he looked around for the first item on the programme. A stir in the wings, and a handsome donkey, decorated with ribbons, was led on to the platform and formally presented to the Earl of Shaftesbury, who laughingly vacated the Chair in its favour. When the clapping subsided he put his arm round the animal's neck and made a short speech of thanks. 'When I have passed away from this life,' he ended, 'I desire to have no more said of me than that I have done my duty, as the poor donkey has done his, with patience and unmurmuring resignation.' As the donkey was led down the steps Shaftesbury remarked, 'And I hope the reporters of the press will state that the donkey having vacated the Chair, the place was taken by Lord Shaftesbury.'

The donkey, 'Coster', was sent to St. Giles's, to the delight of Shaftesbury's grandchildren. When it died after a fall, and was buried 'with all honours in a place I have within a thick plantation, where the pet dogs, horses, etc., that have served the family and deserved our gratitude are gathered together', the costers sent him another, called 'Jack', whom Shaftesbury described as 'the most friendly, useful and sociable creature on the face of the earth'. Whenever Shaftesbury or any of his family was recovering after illness, it was Jack who drew the bath chair.

20

EDUCATION 1870 – THE FATAL FLAW

The annual May meeting of the Ragged School Union was always one of Shaftesbury's happiest occasions.

Long before he entered his brougham for the drive to Exeter Hall the Strand was thick with supporters crowding to get places. Every teacher and every subscriber was a member of the Union; tickets issued to each school and supporting branch totalled more than the available space, and early arrival was essential. Englishmen and women had not yet learned to queue: they pressed towards the doors, 'and even in an Evangelical crowd there can be considerable pressure.'

As the crowd pushed into Exeter Hall, processions of Ragged School children and young people marched down the Strand behind colourful banners. The shoeblack brigades wore their uniforms; some had brass bands and marched in step.

In the hall a great streamer, 'God Bless the Earl of Shaftesbury,' hung above the vast choir space behind the speakers' platform: Exeter Hall was used for choral concerts as well as for public meetings, so the row upon row of tiered seats facing the audience could accommodate all those who were to receive prizes.

Most of the prize-takers were boisterous children or young people. They would be expected to sit through hours of speeches but were excited by the sense of occasion as they took their places. A choirmaster had trained many of them and was holding a last rehearsal, his jokes and patter being laid aside on the great day. Between the choral numbers came exuberance and chatter, and handkerchiefs waving in their hundreds between scholars in the choir seats and supporters in the stalls.

The evening sun filtered through the large windows into the darkening hall. Late arrivals with camp stools squeezed into aisles and corners. When the gaslights came on, the platform seats reserved for the good and great were still empty but the choir area behind made a colourful scene: the tiers marked by brightly embroidered school banners, each one different; the varied uniforms of the shoeblack brigades, the print dresses and white caps of domestic servants whose posts had been found by the schools and now sat together. 'Perpetual motion had reigned since the opening,' wrote one observer, 'and even as the big clock was on the stroke of the hour it seemed hopeless to expect order.'

The first of the platform party entered, to clapping and cheers: first the Ragged School Union officials, then a bishop or a well known Nonconformist. The young looking, red-headed Duke of Argyll, who had long been a devoted supporter and was now a rising statesman, received a specially big cheer. 'But the roar is for the Earl.' The youngsters stamp their feet and cheer themselves hoarse, and Shaftesbury cannot conceal his delight at being with them, while the clapping audience in the well of the hall is thundering its own ovation.

He turns towards the prize-takers and bows gravely to each section, 'with the same elaborate courtesy,' enthused the observer somewhat fancifully, 'that he might have shown to George IV when walking in Hyde Park with the Duke of Wellington.' At last Shaftesbury turns to the audience and bows once, and all are seated and still.

First came prayers. Then the secretary's report, a sore test to the young behind the speaker as they could hear very little: nor, in those days before amplifiers, could many supporters in the back of the stalls or the galleries: they would clap, laugh or wipe their eyes on cue from the front rows who could hear. The young sometimes became a little restless; the earl, as chairman, would pretend not to notice, but occasionally looked round gravely and the murmurs would cease.

Lord Shaftesbury's own speech was never too long by the standards of the day. He always included a reminder of the thousands of destitute or ragged children still unreached, and a warning against the secularisation of England. Then came the resolutions and votes of thanks by speakers of the evening. Some of them were well known orators, others enthusiastic younger supporters or visitors from abroad: D. L. Moody, aged thirty and not yet famous, addressed the R.S.U. meeting in 1867. He had earlier spoken at the Sunday School Union, moving the vote of thanks in a way which much amused Shaftesbury: 'And now about this vote of thanks to the "noble Earl". I don't see why we should thank him any more than he should thank us!' The audience gasped; Shaftesbury's sense of humour was tickled. Five years later when the great campaigns began, Moody had learned to avoid such solecisms.

During the speeches Shaftesbury usually sat with eyes closed and a bored expression. But those on the platform who knew him well could not resist watching him. Charles Montague, an ex-ragged boy, now a respectable tradesman and an R.S.U. council member, knew that if a speaker began to climb oratorical heights towards the precipice 'where pathos may drop into bathos', Shaftesbury would open his eyes. 'The heavy lids opened, while he waited and feared. The danger passed, a flicker of a smile was exchanged with some platform companion whose eyes he happened to meet. Like most serious men he was a humorist as well; and some of these telepathic jokes reduced those with whom they were exchanged to convulsions behind their handkerchiefs.' If a speaker who was trying the audience too much should turn round as he orated, the bored expression of his noble chairman would snuff him quickly; if the speaker did not turn, he might hear from behind him a firm reminder: 'The children!'

Shaftesbury had other methods too. 'It was a disconcerting experience,' his young Russell cousin recorded, 'just as one was warming to an impressive passage, to feel a vigorous pull at one's coat-tail, and to hear a quick, imperative voice say, in no muffled tone, "My dear fellow, are you never going to stop? We shall be here all night."'

A speaker who was always allowed free rein, Judge Payne had the gift of lightening the longest evening by his witty stories and improvised verses. He and Shaftesbury shared many platforms each year and had made a pact: Shaftesbury would laugh or smile at Payne's jokes, and Payne look interested at Shaftesbury's facts, however familiar they were to each other.

After the speeches came the prize-taking. Good-attendance prizes had already been distributed at the schools but youths and girls who had won a prize for holding a first situation, with good conduct, for twelve months, were marched school by school or brigade by brigade across the platform to shake hands with the chairman. The choir sang while Shaftesbury shook nearly a thousand hands.

Every boy or girl was received as if a Cabinet Minister or a peeress. Whether they emigrated to win wealth or fame in the Colonies, or pursued a steady trade in a backstreet at home, they would never forget Lord Shaftesbury's handshake and smile.

* * *

When Shaftesbury returned home after the prize-giving of 1869 he described it as a 'heart-cheering, heart-comforting sight, the result of 25 years of anxiety, labour and prayer'; but he 'wept to think how soon it must pass away'. Gladstone's Government was preparing for state education.

Shaftesbury wanted every child in the land to be taught, and he accepted that a national system must come; but he feared it would 'eliminate all religion and freeze up the flow of genuine, simple evangelical life'. And the Ragged Schools would stop, which would 'greatly abridge my labours but half break my heart'. They had taken root in the land, reaching down where public schools, grammar schools and the numerous other church and voluntary schools could not penetrate. Ragged Schools had lessened crime in the great cities and made London safer; they had developed many means of rescue, welfare and training; they had helped to break barriers between classes; they had proved a powerful means of spreading religion and morality among the poorest. All this looked threatened. 'Ragged Schools,' he recalled seven years later to Lord Sandon, 'fell rapidly and like ninepins the very instant it was declared that the State intended to meddle with Education and substitute the compulsory for the voluntary principle.'

Gladstone's President of the Board of Education, W. E. Forster, then decided to create the system of national education around existing schools rather than sweeping all away to start afresh. The Board of Education would take over any which did not reach an approved standard, but only build 'Board Schools' where necessary. The Ragged Schools need not disappear. Moreover, some years must pass before enough schools could be built to make education compulsory, and these could be filled by a surge of endowing and building of voluntary schools which gave a sympathy and a parental care missing in Board Schools, and where the Christian religion could be taught as part of the curriculum. Shaftesbury mourned that this opportunity was lost because the times were hard and private charity was inclined to dry up if the State would pay.

Shaftesbury feared that a State system must be a secular system; but Forster, a Quaker, wanted his Education Bill of 1870 to allow the teaching of religion in the Board Schools. A great debate immediately began throughout the country. The very intensity of feelings about the 'Religious Question' was a gauge of the advance of Christianity in England during the previous forty years. The National Education Union was founded to ensure that every child had a legal right to the Bible and religious teaching. Another body fought to exclude them, and none could tell how the Commons would vote.

On 8 April 1870 Shaftesbury presided at an enthusiastic

demonstration. With Lord Salisbury, the future Prime Minister, beside him, he made an impassioned speech. Still a strikingly handsome figure, his black hair and whiskers little touched by grey although he was nearly sixty-nine, he stood with a foolscap of notes in his hand, his back straight, his gaunt face lit by fervour for a subject which deeply engaged him, when he could always carry his audience by the warmth and reach of his voice and by an easy choice of words. 'What we ask,' he said, 'is simply this: that the Bible, and the teaching of the Bible to the children of this vast Empire, shall be an essential and not an extra. That religious teaching shall be carried on *within* school hours . . .'

They should insert conscience clauses to satisfy any who wanted to withdraw but he was sure the people of England would never require them. 'What! Exclude by Act of Parliament religious teaching from schools founded, supported, by public rates! Declare that the revealed Word of God and religious teaching shall be exiled to the odds and ends of time, and that only at such periods shall any efforts be devoted to the *most important part of the education of the Youth of this Empire*! It is an outrage upon the national feelings . . .'

He dismissed the very idea in the strongest terms and called on the men and women of England, in his peroration, to rise up and say: 'By all our hopes and by all our fears, by the honour of the nation, by the safety of the people, by all that is holy and all that is true, by everything in time and everything in eternity, the children of Great Britain *shall* be brought up in the faith and fear and nurture of the Lord!' He sat down to a storm of applause. His speech was a powerful factor in checking secularists and those Dissenters who feared that religious teaching would give an advantage to the Church of England, and had therefore wanted to exclude it altogether.

Thenceforth it was agreed that religion should be in the time-table. But the Churches quarrelled bitterly over how it should be taught. To Shaftesbury's sorrow and disgust they lost their opportunity to create an agreed syllabus which should teach, in clear terms, the basic facts of the Christian Faith.

Finally William Cowper-Temple, Minny's brother who had inherited Broadlands under the terms of Palmerston's will, came up with a compromise, which Shaftesbury accepted as the best in the circumstances, and so did all the parties. This famous 'Cowper-Temple clause' laid down that every Board School should teach pupils a knowledge of the Bible but not according to the formularies of any one Church. Thus teachers could interpret the Bible in any way, provided that it did not conform to any Church; the result was 'such a meagre, washy, pointless thing,' concluded Shaftesbury, 'that though thinking people might complain of what was left out, no living soul could make a grievance of what was left in.'

Shaftesbury saw at once, more clearly than many contemporaries, that the Education Act of 1870 would lead to the secularisation of England. The State system would become more powerful than voluntary and church schools and would produce generations with less and less vital Christianity: 'ten thousand are taught to read, not one hundred will be taught to know that there is a God.' The vigorous and practical faith which characterised the later nineteenth century would have lost its force by the mid-twentieth. Most of his friends could only see progress: the surge of church building, missions and social work, the acceptance of the Christian ethic even by those who lacked personal Christian faith: goodness had become fashionable. Shaftesbury saw far farther. He could not know about the immigration of Muslims and Hindus, nor did he foresee the posthumous influence of Karl Marx, writing in obscurity in the British Museum; but Shaftesbury's mournful prophecy would be proved accurate.

'Well, the Education Bill is passed,' he wrote in a brief note to William Cowper-Temple on 5 August 1870. 'It was inevitable; but you will date, from it, the greatest moral change that England has ever known.'

21

DOUBLE GRIEF

'I am going to have here, tomorrow, a regular tea fight. I have invited sixty heads of missions, in the lower parts of London, to come and give me information respecting the progress of Christianity under those forms. Lots of sandwiches, tea, coffee, cakes, bread and butter, and plenty of speeches.' Shaftesbury was writing to Minny on 21 March 1872. He was sitting by a warm fire and had lit a candle although the clock had struck one o'clock in the afternoon.

Snow was falling in Grosvenor Square. It was fortunate that Constance, 'my precious Conty,' their twenty-six year old third daughter, was in the sunshine of the south of France, for her lungs were diseased. When Shaftesbury had come sadly back to London Minny had stayed on at Mentone with Conty and the youngest daughter, Edith, who was always known as Hilda (Shaftesbury gave nicknames to all his children, grandchildren and closest friends). Evelyn's delightful but ailing wife, Sybella (Sissy) was with them, as well as the family parrot and the pugs, for this was before quarantine laws. Shaftesbury kept in touch by letter, writing amusingly about family affairs and seriously about politics and his innumerable concerns.

The tea on 22 March was a great success in helping mission leaders to encourage each other to reach out farther. Among those present, with such stalwarts as George Holland and Orsman the costers' friend, was young Barnardo who gave a graphic account of discovering destitute children on the rooftops: Barnardo long afterwards romanticised this tea into a dinner party followed by a nocturnal voyage of discovery, with Shaftesbury exclaiming as they found children sleeping rough: 'All London shall know of this.' The words were for many years a part of the Barnardo legend, but unless invented they were probably Shaftesbury's comment at Grosvenor Square to emphasise that child destitution, his concern for thirty years, remained.

Another impassioned speaker was Catherine Booth, deputising for her husband William Booth, both still in their thirties. She described their work in the roughest parts of the East End for the past six years, saving souls and bodies. At the tea Shaftesbury had said in his welcome: 'Your plans must be aggressive that you may go and take by storm these people in their lairs,' but when Booth, six years later, renamed his 'Christian Mission' the Salvation Army, assumed the title of General and began to take pagan lairs by storm, Shaftesbury disapproved of their flamboyance and 'spiritual gymnastics'. A stalwart of one generation does not always appreciate a stalwart of the next, but Shaftesbury would be quick in support during the last months of his life, when the Booths' eldest son attacked by original means a horror which Shaftesbury had long fought but had found no way to crush.

*   *   *

On 10 June 1872, their forty-second wedding anniversary, Shaftesbury rhapsodised: 'What a faithful, devoted, simple-hearted and captivating wife she has been, and is to me! And what a mother!' He and 'that dear, beautiful, true and affectionate darling' were still apart for another week as Minny journeyed slowly home with the invalid Conty.

Hardly had they come together in London when the doctor ordered Conty to Malvern, as the only hope of saving her life. Nursing her devotedly Minny overtaxed her strength and fell dangerously ill with asthma, but seemed to revive. Shaftesbury wrote on 30 September to ask the costers at the Golden Lane mission 'to aid me by their prayers. My wife and daughter have been very ill; and there is still danger. I believe much in the prayers of Christian people; and I know that there are many among you – so do not forget me. Our Lord teaches us that there is mighty power in the fervent supplications of the poor. The children, too, must remember me, as I have often remembered them.'

Orsman received the letter as he left for a coster wedding. He read it out. One of the costers immediately called the others to silent prayer 'for these dear ones', but the answer was not as Shaftesbury so strongly desired. At noon on 15 October 1872 Minny died at Grosvenor Square. She was not quite sixty-two. Shaftesbury nearly broke under the shock. His black hair, of which he had been a little proud when he reached seventy, turned grey.

Waves of sympathy flowed in, and he was much comforted by a letter in her own hand from the widowed Queen, which has not previously been published: '*Balmoral*, Oct. 19. 1872. The Queen recd yesterday Lord Shaftesbury's sad letter & wishes in thanking him for it, to express her deep sympathy with him in his present terrible infliction. He cd not, she trusts for a moment doubt of what her feelings must be considering for how many years she has known him & *her* whom he mourns, & how many ties of friendship bound her to his dear wife's family.

'How well, from the Queen's earliest years has she known Lord and Lady Shaftesbury, & has seen their children grow up, & how sad it is to see the departure of so many of the family within the last 12 years!

'The Queen wd ask Lord Shaftesbury to say every thing most kind & feeling to his bereaved children from her & to believe that she feels most truly for them & him, & prays that God may support & comfort them as only He can.'

The doctors ordered Conty's immediate return to the south of France. Before he set out with her on the slow journey he was down at The Saint for the first time since the funeral. The house seemed 'sad, solitary and silent . . . When dark, crept into the church and prayed to God in peace, though not in happiness near her dear resting place.'

At Mentone, Constance rallied, and then in mid-December she had a final relapse. Victorian death-beds were drawn-out affairs, and consumption provided some of the most sentimental of them through the curious brilliance it gave to face and feelings. But the English nurse, who said she had attended many true Christians at death, had 'never seen anything approaching to this. I can only call it angelic.'

'Never was a death so joyous, so peaceful,' said Shaftesbury, 'she taught me more in one half-hour than I had imparted to her in her whole life.' When Cecil quoted, 'To me to live is Christ, and to die is gain,' Constance cried with a happy fervour which almost startled Shaftesbury, 'Oh yes, yes, thank you, thank you . . . Christ is very near.'

22

'I MUST WORK AS LONG AS LIFE LASTS'

In Minny's memory Shaftesbury set up the 'Emily Loan Fund' for girls selling flowers and watercress in London streets. Out of season they had no means to support themselves but now could borrow and eventually buy a potato oven or a whelk stall, coffee barrow or other tools for a winter trade. The Watercress and Flower Girls' Mission had been founded by John Groom; Shaftesbury wrote to a friend: 'I cannot describe to you half the good that this association has done to the bodies and souls of thousands of poor *defenceless girls.*' He also supported John Groom's Crippleage which became the more famous enterprise.

Without Minny, Shaftesbury in his seventies was more prone to gloom and fears, yet he turned his grief into deeper sympathy for all who suffered. As he said to the Westminster poor at their next annual flower show in Dean's Yard: 'The great and final Garden of Paradise is only to be approached through the Garden of Gethsemane.' Sometimes melancholy and loneliness almost submerged him. 'Who is with me?' was now a frequent theme of his diary, though hundreds worked with him and the toiling millions loved him: a few years earlier, when he was ill and wrongly reported as dying, no less than four hundred people kept vigil outside his house in Grosvenor Square.

The diary continued to be a means, with prayer and the Bible, by which he faced his conflicts and found balance before he went out into the world, where he did not exude gloom, apart from gloomy pronouncements, either among his family or to the public, but rather a venerable kindliness. Once he was walking along crowded Oxford Street, noisy with the rattle of carriages and carts and omnibuses and the horses' hooves on the cobbles, when he noticed ahead a little girl standing timidly on the edge of the pavement. She looked up at several passers-by but each time shook her head. As he approached she came timidly towards him. 'Please, sir, will you see me across the road?' He took her hand firmly and together they braved the traffic. Shaftesbury said in telling the story that her request was one of the nicest compliments ever paid him. Legend has added that he asked why she chose him and she replied: 'Because you have such a kind face.'

Sustained by his faith he plunged back into work. The years after Minny's death were some of his most strenuous. These were the years of his fight for the children in the brickfields, of the final liberation of the chimney boys; of helping the difficult Plimsoll, always his own worst enemy, to achieve reforms for seafarers. At this time also the co-operative Artisans, Labourers and General Dwellings Company, of which Shaftesbury was president, built Shaftesbury Park in south west London, the first 'new town' of model houses, followed by Queen's Park near Shepherd's Bush. He had longed for such a scheme and laid the foundation stone; but when the enterprise was nearly ruined by the dishonesty of the manager he gladly let his son Evelyn, now M.P. for Poole, take on with others the burden of rescue.

Shaftesbury continued to speak in Parliament and on the platform about the great political issues of the day, such as the Irish Question, Electoral Reform, and India: after he had opposed the Royal Titles Bill which made Queen Victoria Empress of India, Disraeli complained to the Queen, unfairly, that 'Lord Shaftesbury is always ready to place philanthropy at the aid of faction.'

Shaftesbury was much engaged in Church reform. Whether his judgments in detail were right or wrong, his whole being centred round Christ and the Bible. 'My invariable guide was never to go in action or belief where the Scriptures would not guide me. This never failed me.' Justification by Faith, 'that grand doctrine, the very life of the Bible', was to him 'the great saving truth, without which no other truth in Scripture would be worth having – salvation by a crucified Redeemer.' Prayer was the breath of his daily life, and his special comfort still lay in the certainty of Christ's Second Coming. The text, in Greek, 'Even so, come, Lord Jesus,' was embossed on the flaps of his envelopes. 'There is no real remedy for all this mass of misery,' he would say, 'but in the return of our Lord Jesus Christ. Why do we not plead for it every time we hear the clock strike?'

In March 1875 Moody and Sankey, the American evangelists, came to London after successful missions in Scotland and the provinces. Shaftesbury was somewhat surprised not to be asked to help, like Lord Chancellor Cairns; nor was he invited to the preparatory reception. When they began their mission at the Agricultural Hall in Islington, seating 15,000, he was a little cautious, basing his views on inaccurate newspaper reports; but soon he was writing: 'It looks amazingly like the "right man at the right hour".'

Next day, Good Friday, he went for the first time and gladly admitted that they 'preach Christ crucified' – he had heard that they ignored the Cross. 'Deeply impressed,' he wrote, 'the more impressed because of the imperfection of the whole thing.' Sankey's song went 'to the inmost soul, and seemed to empty it of everything, but thought of the good, tender, and lowly Shepherd'. Moody's voice was 'bad and ill managed, the language colloquial, yet the result is striking, effective, touching and leading to much thought . . . the Holy Spirit can work out of feeble materials. Is it not so today?'

Shaftesbury put his prestige and experience fully behind the mission. 'Why,' he said at the annual meeting of the C.P.A.S., 'what are Messrs Moody and Sankey doing but acting on the very thing which I advocated – the enlisting of the working man. Mr. Moody had a wonderful power of getting at the hearts of the people. It is Christ with him, and nothing but Christ: He preaches Christ simply . . .'

At a discussion of committee and sympathisers on the morning of 7 April, Shaftesbury more than anyone directed Moody to the scene of his most remarkable influence in London.

Moody would shortly begin in the East End, preaching in a huge gas-lit temporary structure to the working poor. He would also give morning Bible readings in a West End opera house for the leisured rich. In addition he planned to continue in Islington beyond schedule, thus preaching twice each night until he started in south London. But Shaftesbury, 'in a most earnest and powerful appeal to Mr. M.', urged evening meetings in the West End: 'In the Opera House your preaching will be heard by multitudes who will throng in of an evening from the university clubs, the naval and military and other clubs in the neighbourhood. There will be many of high intellectual and social position who will thus have the Gospel brought nearer to them, and not only these but many tradesmen and shopkeepers and their dependents who cannot or will not go to Islington.'

Moody demurred, but the success of the West End morning Bible readings convinced him that Shaftesbury was right, and he dashed each evening from Bow Common to the Haymarket to preach in the Queen's Opera House. 'The scene in the Haymarket baffles description,' wrote an eye-witness. 'It was literally blocked with the carriages of the aristocratic and plutocratic of the land; and the struggle for admission was perhaps more severe in the West than in the East.'

One of the converts at the Opera House was a wealthy retired planter from India, Edward Studd. His new-found faith was soon the means of the conversion of his three sons, schoolboys at Eton. Ten years later one of the sons, C. T. Studd, had become the greatest all-round cricketer of the day when he astonished the world by giving up all his prospects in order to be a missionary in China, one of the young men of wealth and athletic fame who became known as the Cambridge Seven and profoundly touched their generation.

*   *   *

All this time Shaftesbury had unending demands on his time. Each morning from eleven to one he was at home in Grosvenor Square to any who sought his aid and advice. The first caller might be the secretary of one of his societies, the next a deputation of mutilated miners to consult him about the enforcement of the law in their pits. They went away heartened by his sympathy and girded by careful advice. Once, 'a great burglar wanted to see me.' He talked of a number of things, then he urged: 'Keep hold of the little 'uns. You can't help us, we're too far gone, but save the little 'uns.' If Ragged Schools had existed 'when I was a lad', he would never have turned to crime.

Often the callers were men or women who wanted to start a new mission or expand an old one. Shaftesbury always made careful enquiries; if satisfied he would accept the presidency, which involved yet another donation although he was hard-pressed for money: as he once commented, 'Philanthropy, with a peerage, reduces a man to the lowest point.'

When he hung up his coat at the House of Lords he would find a pile of letters and petitions from all parts of the kingdom on all manner of subjects, waiting in a recess of one of the windows overlooking the Thames. He frequently complained in the diary at his vast correspondence but he never wanted a full-time private secretary for long, nor could he afford one. Occasionally he asked John Matthias Weylland, an official of the London City Mission, to weed out letters which needed no reply and to give him the gist of those which did. One of the family usually wrote out the file copies and sometimes the original reply at his dictation, but he preferred to answer letters in his own hand, reading them quickly and writing fast with a quill. He stood at a tall desk, still preserved at St. Giles's, until old age forced him to sit.

When he returned at night from the House or from chairing a meeting or perhaps from a dinner engagement, he might find several of the poor on his doorstep. He would always invite them in and listen to their troubles. Weylland once urged him to shelter himself from such late applicants. Shaftesbury opened a drawer and drew out a photograph of an old lady with a cheerful, well dressed girl of sixteen or eighteen at her side.

'You think so, do you?' said Shaftesbury with that rather cold dignity which he adopted whenever someone tried to stop him. 'But if I so acted, I should, by neglect, injure the poor who have no helper. You see this sweet girl! Well, one cold night, when only four years old, she was brought by a poor man to my door, cold and starving. We took her in, and next day placed her in a Home. She was sent to Canada with a batch of friendless ones. This lady took her into her service, educated her, and has now adopted her as her daughter. Their grateful letters make me glad that I am a living man.'

*   *   *

Shaftesbury loved going down to The Saint during the Parliamentary Recess, lonely though it must always have been without Minny. Vea had made a happy marriage with the widowed Lord Templemore so that Hilda was now the only daughter at home. Sons came and went, and to Shaftesbury's great delight Accy's wife had abandoned her antagonism. He had been upset when Harriet came under the influence of the Tractarian, G. H. Wilkinson, vicar of St. Peter's, Eaton Square, and first Bishop of Truro, 'that Arch Jesuit'; but Harriet not only became a religious woman but affectionate towards her father-in-law. She no longer kept her children away.

The youngest daughter of Accy and Harriet was then a small girl. Fifty years later Lady Maud Warrender recalled her grandfather as 'a magnificent and rather melancholy figure, six feet tall and with thick grey hair, but with a solemn sense of humour that bubbled forth at times and betrayed itself by a rather remote twinkle in his great blue eyes.

'He loved to tell of the amusing things that happened to him in his philanthropic career. The humorous side of him has never been recorded by his biographers, only the pious and serious side.

'For instance, he was once taking the Chair at a meeting of some charitable society, and through some mistake *nobody* turned up but himself and one newspaper reporter. Getting up he said: "At this large and distinguished meeting . . ." The reporter looked up wonderingly. "Why not?" said the Chairman. "It's true. Am I not large, and are you not distinguished?"

'Having satisfied himself with this they both walked out!'

St. Giles's was not stately on the scale of Chatsworth or Castle Howard but for Shaftesbury it was home. Though he had to sell some of the pictures, and preferred to spend money on philanthropy, he looked after it lovingly. He lowered the level of the lake to stop damp getting into the house, tamed the weed and improved the cascade: 'I have been very anxious to retain the lake. It is an important feature of the place, admired by all who see it, and a special favourite with members of the family.' He preserved the famous shell grotto of 1750, restored the Elizabethan stables, and catalogued the library himself, as time allowed.

His favourite room was not the state dining room with its full-length family portraits, or the billiard room, hung with tapestries, or the drawing room with its magnificent carved gilt side-tables in the form of eagles, commissioned by the philosopher third earl; but a smaller room, opening out on to the lawn, which he had turned into what he called his 'den'. It had his escritoire, several tables piled with Parliamentary papers, transactions of learned societies, and mission reports; his dressing table; and in a corner a narrow low iron bedstead, almost as spartan as the one used by the hero of his youth, the Great Duke. Shaftesbury's bed quilt was a multicoloured patchwork of serge, like a cottage hearthrug. It had been made and presented to him as a

horse-cloth by boys of a Ragged School. 'No, my lads,'
Shaftesbury had said in accepting it, 'not for a horse-cloth.
It shall cover me at night as long as I live.' He would tell
visitors: 'I am comfortable under it as I feel near to the poor
boys.'

John Weylland, the former City missionary, born in a
humble home, much admired the stately rooms when he
stayed at The Saint, but it was the 'den' which impressed
him most: 'It was in this room that the secret of Lord
Shaftesbury's conquering faith and power for well-doing
could be discovered. It was here that in the early morning
he studied his Bible, and held communion with his God. He
was a morning reader of the Word, and this gave him
strength and freshness for the many and weary duties of
the day.'

Shaftesbury liked to go for a walk in the grounds before
breakfast, first filling his pockets with pieces of bread from a
bag kept behind the library door. As he approached the
lake, wild fowl would swoop towards him and ducks
waddle up to be fed. He claimed that whenever he arrived
at St. Giles's, even after a six months' absence, the wild
birds would fly round him in welcome.

The household and family gathered in the dining room
for family prayers: if the sons cut, he would be disappointed and suspect decline in faith. He read the Scriptures with warmth, bringing out the meaning by his tones,
and prayed set prayers, often of his own composition, with
a deep reverence. Family prayers were quite short. The
doors were then opened and the dogs would bound in. For
Bible lessons to the grandchildren the dogs stayed: he
would end by shutting the Bible with a bang and they all
barked.

At dinner in the evening Shaftesbury allowed the dogs to
attend the first two courses. 'After taking his seat,' recalls
Weylland, 'two great dogs, one a Scotch collie, entered, and
with an amusing look of importance used to take their
places at each side, their jaws upon his knees. He would
caress them, and after the second course give each a piece of
meat, and then utter the command, "Now be off." At this,

with an affectionate look into his face and with wagging of
the tail, they went out with reluctant tread.'

Weylland was entranced by Shaftesbury's conversation
at these dinner parties. 'It was entertaining and at times
brilliant. All branches of knowledge were at his command,
and from the store of his retentive memory he brought
narratives of great variety; stories of kings, emperors,
statesmen, and distinguished persons of the past and present generation, were in rich abundance, while flashes of
wit and humour made him all but bewitching.

'We well remember one occasion when he had been
fascinating, light-hearted, and humorous to excess. At
length the other gentlemen left to join the ladies, and we
remained behind to settle a contention. He rose from the
chair, and, leaning upon the massive mantelpiece, thought
for a moment. Then came the rebound: "I enjoy," he said,
"the fun and the word-frolic of the table, but my thoughts
soon revert to the desire of the heart. There are not two
hours in the day, but I think of the second advent of our
Lord. That is the hope of the church, for Israel and the
world. Come, Lord Jesus, come quickly." And then we
entered the drawing-room to enjoy a musical evening –
one of his home delights.'

*   *   *

St. Giles's was not a holiday. The estate, though now
managed by the excellent Turnbull, took much time; county
business as Lord Lieutenant required attention; many of
the guests at The Saint had come down for work on one or
other of Shaftesbury's concerns.

Every August he went abroad to Ems or Homburg to
'drink the waters', still the doctors' favourite cure for
digestive ills, if the patient could afford it. He would take
some of the family, who found the routine, the company
and the food equally wearisome; even the new game of
lawn tennis was fatiguing to Hilda on an August afternoon
at Homburg.

It was here in 1878 that Shaftesbury broke the rules about

Royalty. Princess Mary Adelaide, Duchess of Teck, the large and large hearted granddaughter of George III and mother of the future Queen Mary, had arrived and the four Shaftesburys were bidden to dine at the Kurhaus.

After dinner the bulky Princess did not wish to follow custom and walk about the gardens, 'so she sits on for ever,' wrote Hilda to Syssie. 'We dined at 6.30 and at 9 o'clock we were still sitting there. Everybody was casting despairing looks at each other, and swearing inwardly.' No one may move before Royalty. Lionel, sitting opposite his father, who was next to the Princess, 'had been on thorns for some time, for Papa kept giving all sorts of hints pulling out his watch and telling her that it was getting very late etc.!'

Princess Mary had no sense of time and was notoriously unpunctual. She remained unaware of any discomfort or waste of an evening for her distinguished 77-year-old neighbour. 'At last, after 9 o'clock Papa, to the horror of Col. Greville (who is of course a courtier) but to the amusement of everybody else, got up, wished Princess Mary Goodnight and walked off. Even then she sat on . . .'

Shaftesbury left Homburg with joy, for his real holiday was in Scotland every September. He had become great friends with George Burns and his son John (later Lord Inverclyde), founders of the Cunard Steamship Company. When he stayed with Hilda at the Burns' opulent homes at Wemyss Bay, west of Glasgow, all his cares seemed to melt away. He loved the Burns family for their humour, their deep faith and their love of the Jewish people and hope of the Jews' return to Palestine, the hope that had never died in Shaftesbury's heart.

The Burnses took him on cruises up the sea lochs in their yacht. They took him deep-sea fishing too, according to a newly discovered letter from another of Shaftesbury's closest friends, Alexander Haldane, editor of *The Record*, to his son. They left him undisturbed to walk about the terraces and lawns of their two adjoining mansions, Wemyss House and Castle Wemyss, which stood high on a rock above the sea. Here Burns the Younger placed a suite of rooms at his disposal. Shaftesbury felt so free that he even shocked his own valet, Goldsmith, by refusing to dress for dinner when eighteen were expected. 'I am at Castle Wemyss!' he roared as if announcing a hymn in Exeter Hall. At Castle Wemyss it was proverbial that 'wherever the ripple of laughter was to be heard and the most fun going on, there Lord Shaftesbury was invariably to be found.'

One day he was sitting on the lawn with old George Burns, looking across the Firth of Clyde to the hills. Suddenly he said: 'If I followed my own inclination I would sit in my armchair and take it easy for the rest of my life. But I dare not do it. I must work as long as life lasts.'

23

AGE AND HONOUR

The approaches to the Guildhall in the City of London had known many scenes of pomp and circumstance but none so unusual as the arrival of gaily decorated donkeys and barrows, carrying happy parties of costermongers, their wives and children, in pearly best. They ranged themselves behind the barriers in Guildhall Yard and clapped and cheered or threw witty comments as distinguished guests alighted from their carriages on the afternoon of Thursday 28 April 1881 – the eightieth birthday of Lord Shaftesbury.

Many of those arriving were not in the least distinguished: Ragged School teachers and scholars, shoeblacks in their uniforms, City missionaries, committee members or workers from scores of religious and philanthropic societies. The Ragged School Union were to present their president with his portrait, and the Lord Mayor, a strong Christian himself, had offered the Guildhall because the Mansion House proved too small for all who wanted tickets.

Guildhall Yard was packed with East Enders and Londoners of all kinds to welcome the guest of honour. As his carriage drove up they made the buildings echo with their cheers. Vea and Hilda stepped down, and then the Earl, and the cheering grew deafening. His face might look melancholy in repose but now it was lit by his smile as he doffed his top hat to coster after coster and to the crowds. He entered the Guildhall. Girls from the Flower Girls'

Mission strewed spring flowers in front of him all the way
to the platform as he walked, leaning on his stick. At his
appearance the entire assembly rose and sang the Doxo-
logy. Soon afterwards the Lord Mayor and Lady Mayoress,
in full robes, escorted by mace and sword bearer, entered
the hall.

Behind the platform rose a dais with tiers of crimson
seats, specially erected for the more important guests. Yet
as Shaftesbury heard the apologies for absence, he felt that
the poor of the land had been slighted: the Prime Minister,
Gladstone, could not find the time; no archbishop, not even
a bishop, though Spurgeon had come; no men of science,
art or literature.

The Liberal Foreign Secretary, his old friend and some-
time opponent, Earl Granville, would have proposed the
resolution but was ill. It was proposed by the young Earl of
Aberdeen, conscious that Shaftesbury hated flattery, yet
finding no way to avoid eulogy; and seconded by a Cabinet
minister, W. E. Forster, famous for the Education Act of
1870.

Forster was a Bradford mill owner, though born in
Dorset, and when he praised the great changes brought by
the Factory Acts, he spoke from experience. He added:
'Lord Shaftesbury would be the very first to reproach me if I
said that all this improvement in the factory and mining
industries is solely due to him.' The audience heard the
guest of honour give a loud, 'Hear, Hear,' and Forster went
on: 'He laughs at the very notion that he could have done it
alone.' Forster mentioned Oastler and others but he said
that Shaftesbury's was the household name in the north:
'There are many homesteads in the villages and towns of
Yorkshire in which the father and mother will remember
how Lord Ashley saved them from almost destructive and
killing work.'

Shaftesbury in his response spoke mostly of the great
achievements of the Ragged Schools – at least 300,000 children had been taken off the streets and turned into useful
citizens. He warned of 'the terrible depths yet to be
fathomed of ignorance and misery'. Among all the

speeches that afternoon, however, the words of an obscure Londoner best summed up Shaftesbury's eighty years.

J. M. Clabon had served under his direction as secretary of a Reformatory for Adult Male Criminals, who were received on discharge, taught a trade and found jobs at home or abroad. Clabon said: 'I think there is no man of this, if of any other century, who has deserved such thanks as the noble earl. The myriads of children who from the tenderest age were kept standing for sixteen hours a day in hot factories – the poor half-clad women who, harnessed to cars in coal mines, used to draw them along low, dark passages – the gutter children of London and all great towns – the uncared-for lunatic – the prisoner in the foreign dungeon – the oppressed of every clime – owe him thanks for exemption from misery. And inasmuch as he did it to all these, he did it to the Saviour whom he always loved so well.'

The Times, reporting the meeting, commented that 'It is given to few men to see so completely the fruit of their labours as he has done. To have changed the whole social condition of England, to have emancipated women and children from a condition almost worse than slavery, to have reclaimed the neglected and regenerated the outcast, – these are results which give the aged philanthropist a foremost place among those who have laboured for the welfare of England.'

His initiatives had been followed. University Settlements, public school missions; Dr. Barnardo's and other orphanages; training institutes, holiday homes, philanthropies of all kinds were springing up. British Governments now showed a sensitivity to social needs which would have puzzled Lord Melbourne. The Factory Acts were being extended; indeed the Liberal Party was already claiming credit for reforms which Shaftesbury had won against the opposition of many of its leading members. But, as Shaftesbury had said in his speech, complacency could not be allowed: there was much to be done.

He would not give up. Over eighty, growing deaf and with his eyes weak, he continued to intervene in all the great questions of the day, whether from his place in the House of Lords, or by private letter to a statesman or public letter to *The Times*. He was quick to respond to oppression or injustice. When, in 1882, the Tsarist Government began a violent onslaught on the Jews in Russia, he became president of a relief committee to raise funds to help Jews who wished to emigrate to western Europe, or to Cyprus since the Turkish Government would not have them in Palestine. The committee took an office near the Houses of Parliament so that Shaftesbury could look in on his way to the Lords. The daughter of his old friend 'Rabbi' McCaul was the leading spirit, and in her old age she recalled Shaftesbury 'attending almost every meeting and taking the deepest personal interest in the work'.

His voice could no longer always reach to the far end of a great hall, though it retained the timbre and warmth which made his speeches so effective. He was always ready to visit Ragged Schools and open new refuges or homes. He presided over the meeting in April 1883 to lay the plans which eventually developed the Ragged School Union into the Shaftesbury Society, still working for children. He chaired the Luther Commemoration, he unveiled statues of William Tyndale, the Bible translator, and Robert Raikes, founder of Sunday Schools. He became the very active president of the newly formed Anti-Vivisection Society and supported the Cremation Society in their efforts to overcome widespread social and religious prejudice: cremation was almost unknown in England. And always the Lunacy Commission took time, especially as he opposed the Liberal Lord Chancellor's new Bill, and resigned, but resumed the chair after the Government fell and the Bill was dropped.

To most of his fellow-workers, and to the poor, his life seemed to be enjoying a sunset glow but in the privacy of his den he suffered bouts of almost overwhelming depression. The hereditary tendency,[1] deepened by the scars

1. His eldest son committed suicide six months after succeeding to the title, mentally unbalanced by depression caused by a wrong belief that he faced financial ruin.

of his miserable childhood, was compounded by tiredness as he struggled to meet every request for aid or advice or the sympathy he loved to give. If a good plan for the poor or afflicted should be opposed, he could be outwardly cold, even angry, but in his heart he cried out or mourned. And his awareness of the suffering of others had not lessened with old age. He seemed to walk so often in the Garden of Gethsemane.

Yet he could throw off sadness. 'We were delighted with Lord Shaftesbury's visit,' wrote a Manchester rector in July 1883 to George Burns. 'He was so well, so vigorous and so happy, and the ovation he received at the Free Trade Hall was so singular a demonstration of hearty and grateful respect for the man to whom Lancashire especially, but the whole country owes so much.

'The vast and packed crowd in the Free Trade Hall on Monday night behaved splendidly. The representatives of the various Christian work for the children of the poor – Refuges, Industrial and Ragged Schools – spoke admirably, and when one who was himself a ragged boy, found in Charter's Street and taken to school – now a respectable and Christian citizen, in good position, came forward to present the magnificently illuminated and framed address (which was carried to the platform by four children), the interest reached its climax. There were many eyes moist while "Mr. Thomas Johnson," this ragged boy grown into an excellent and useful citizen, addressed Lord S. in plain, natural, and deeply grateful and affectionate words.

'I wish I could have photographed the scene when Lord Shaftesbury came forward and grasped that honest man's hand, accepting in the same spirit the loving gratitude of the representatives of his class. Lord S. said it was not given to many men to have such feelings as that grand meeting and its proceedings awakened in his bosom.'

In June 1884 he received the Freedom of the City of London – a very overdue honour. Glasgow had given him its Freedom thirteen years before, in scenes of great enthusiasm; civic London seemed to forget that one of the greatest of living Englishmen had been a Londoner by birth

and had done more for its population than any other
contemporary. The aged Shaftesbury allowed himself a
gentle and humorous hint of reproach when he said in the
course of his reply: 'It will be an honour and a pleasure to
me to uphold the rights of the City, and to perform humble
service in the ranks . . . Though the world is closing before
me I confess I rejoice, even at this late period, to be admitted
to the long rolls and ranks of noble and worthy men.' He
trusted that when he died the newspapers would record
'that I died a citizen of London'.

The City made up for tardiness by the splendour of the
gold casket, its design chosen by competition. The decora-
tions included the arms of the City and of the Earldom and
the highly appropriate family motto: *Love, Serve*. On the
reverse was engraved a Bible text and a symbolic picture.
The supporting figures 'represented the classes which have
most needed his Lordship's labour', while those on the top
symbolised the results of his reforms. A guardian angel
hovered above.

*   *   *

That same month Shaftesbury agreed to preside when
Spurgeon's congregation decided to celebrate his fiftieth
birthday, with well-wishers from all denominations, by a
great meeting in his enormous new Metropolitan Taber-
nacle, south of the Thames. The audience had greeted the
Baptist preacher with rapture when a few moments later
'the venerable Earl of Shaftesbury was discerned making
his way to the chair.' They rose *en masse*, cheering and
clapping and waving handkerchiefs. The applause thundered again when he stood to speak. Despite his eighty-
three years his unaided voice was audible throughout.

In the course of a strong address Shaftesbury described
his ideal of preaching which could reach 'that large class of
people untaught in the truths of the Gospel, strangers to
the first principles of religious life'. An easy, colloquial
mode, with illustrations and parables after the 'example of
our Lord . . . is the way to go to the hearts of the people.

Stilted sentences, long periods, high sounding words, and laboured efforts of intellect are foreign to the taste of those whom we aim to teach. They like a religion that goes straight to the heart. A cosy religion and a cosy form of worship suit them. They like prayer that touches their present case, and tells their pressing need. When their instinct feels that you have gripped their weakness on earth, they are ready to believe that you have linked them on to the Omnipotence in heaven.'

Moody and Sankey had just ended their second London Campaign. Shaftesbury was most encouraged by signs of a widespread turning to God in unlikely places, and told the Bible Society's annual meeting in 1884: 'What I am about to say is almost incredible and I dare say those who listen to me who are not very much in the habit of going among the most destitute and degraded classes of the community, will hardly believe me; but in no period of the history of the world was there ever such a movement among the most degraded, the most miserable, and apparently the most abandoned and hopeless class of the community towards a knowledge of the Word of God as there is at present. It is positively the fact that hundreds of the poorer sort – even the very roughest of lads – come to those different institutions with which I am connected, more especially to those in Whitechapel, praying to be admitted to Bible classes.

'I should hardly have thought it possible if I had not seen it with my own eyes and heard it with my own ears. I accept it as the intervention of some very special, notable, and miraculous sign that hundreds and thousands of these poorest of the poor should be brought to such a desire for the knowledge of the Gospel, and should be praying to be admitted into the fold of Christ.'

But he could not forget that they were poor; that slums and destitution were too prevalent still. 'When I feel old age creeping upon me,' he wrote to a friend, 'and know that I must soon die – I hope it is not wrong to say it – I cannot bear to leave this world with all the misery in it.'

24

'OUR EARL'S GONE'

The next winter was a hard one for the poor, but Shaftesbury, who was now seldom without pain, having fallen ill with gastic trouble and chronic diarrhoea on 26 July 1884, could no longer regularly visit the East End of London.

One afternoon, however, he struggled to George Holland's Ragged School and many-sided mission in Whitechapel, where his venerable figure was familiar to the numerous boys and girls. As he walked slowly round the varied activities he noticed one boy who looked ill. Shaftesbury asked what was the matter and cupped his hand to his ear. His lordship was known to be very deaf these days and the boy spoke up: 'I have had no food for some time.' 'How long?' asked Shaftesbury. The boy replied, 'Twenty-six hours.' 'Twenty-six hours! Why you must be fainting; no wonder you look ill.' 'Oh that is nothing,' replied the boy. 'I have gone without two days afore now.'

Child after child had much the same tale (and children did not lie to Shaftesbury) until at last he left the schoolroom and went into one of the small rooms, where Holland found him in tears. Holland, that 'genuine, ardent, lovable and Christ-hearted man', was reduced to mouthing a text: 'My God shall supply all their need.' 'Yes, he will,' replied Shaftesbury, 'they must have some food directly.' He got into his brougham and was driven home.

A few hours later two enormous churns of soup arrived in the earl's carriage, from the earl's kitchen, enough to feed four hundred. And that winter ten thousand basins of soup and bread were distributed to starving children and their parents from the Shaftesbury mansion in Grosvenor Square.

In the spring of 1885 he was unable for the first time to attend the May Meeting of the Ragged School Union; it would have been his forty-first and he had hoped until almost the last minute to preside, at least 'for an hour, if possible'. The assembly sent him an affectionate telegram before opening proceedings with the new hymn from America: 'To God be the Glory, Great things He hath done.' Then George Holland led in prayer.

A week later Shaftesbury was well enough to attend a smaller meeting at Exeter Hall which touched him deeply. Former scholars of Ragged Schools wanted to present him with an illuminated Address, and for each of his surviving children a copy in oils, set in a massive gilt frame, of Holman Hunt's famous picture, *The Light of The World*. Gladstone, still Prime Minister but nearing his fall from power, had promised to be present but had to go to Windsor for a Privy Council.

The meeting had already begun when Shaftesbury, with Accy and the eldest granddaughter, and Evelyn, Lionel, Cecil, Vea and Hilda, 'entered the room and met with a perfect ovation. It is impossible to convey,' runs the report, 'an adequate description of the enthusiasm his presence evoked. The whole meeting rose to its feet and cheered again and again, hats and handkerchiefs being waved as Lord Shaftesbury ascended the platform.' He found it difficult to hear all the nice things that were said or to read very clearly the illuminated writing of the testimonial when they unveiled it with the pictures. He thanked the meeting for their kindness and ended his speech with the words of Bossuet, 'I pray that the rest of my life, whatever its duration, may be consecrated to God's service – "the remains of a voice that is beginning to fail, and of an ardour which is almost extinct."'

Next day he was able to address a drawing room meeting for the Ragged School Union, at the Duke of Westminster's palatial home, Grosvenor House, with a long speech full of stories and memories of the schools to show their influence. They had saved thousands from crime. They had made London a safer place, though much was yet to be done. 'Bad as things are now,' he concluded, 'what would they have been but for the Ragged Schools and other movements springing out of this work? I can say no more, my voice fails. I can only hope you will do all that in you lies to foster this great movement . . .'

A few days later he went down to The Saint. At last, in his den at St. Giles's, with the collies at his feet, he could study the illuminated Address. One of his curious traits was a conviction, all his life, that no one really appreciated him; yet here these once-ragged boys off the streets, now citizens of substance, were telling him what his 'dear and honoured name' meant to them. 'There are literally tens of thousands,' he read, 'to whom your public and private acts have brought comfort and happiness, and in thus helping the helpless you have benefited the whole English-speaking people.'

He pulled out a sheet of paper and wrote to the organis-ers of the Address: 'I must tell you that I am deeply touched by its kind, affectionate, and intimate language and ex-pressions. It has gone to my very heart . . . It is a comfort, a positive comfort for me to learn that any efforts of mine have, under God's special blessing, contributed to start those who signed the paper, on their own part and the part of many others,' in their 'joyous and happy' careers.

Early in June he returned to London. Then he learned, to his astonishment, that a complete stranger named Miss Douglas had left him the then very considerable sum of £60,000 to distribute to the poor at his sole discretion. He had often been given or left sums to distribute, or been invited to guide a would-be philanthropist, but this huge amount would be beyond him at his great age. He sent for Weylland and told him that the anxiety, work and possible legal difficulties had decided him to exercise an option allowed him in the Will: the executors should choose the recipients.

Weylland was silent.

'Why don't you speak?'

Weylland replied that he disagreed but was thinking how best to put across his thoughts.

Shaftesbury smiled. 'You know my weakness for humour, but out with it.'

Weylland then convinced him that he should undertake the task, and obtained leave of the London City Mission to help him. Shaftesbury took endless trouble as he chose hospitals and good causes, drew up and redrew the lists, studied the applications and requests which poured in, or thought of fresh claims, until his strength and emotions almost gave out and Weylland was 'moved to tears at his heroic conflict with weakness.' The old earl would 'stagger to his bedroom for half an hour's rest, returning bright and cheerful.'

Meanwhile the troubles of the Lunacy Commission were plunging him into depression. He would also break off to preside at promised meetings. He managed the flower-girls, and the Westminster Flower Show, but not the costers to his particular distress; and once he actually reached the Duke of Westminster's door for a charity drawing room meeting before turning back. He presided at the meeting which founded the Gordon Home for Boys as a national memorial to General Gordon, killed at Khartoum. In July he spoke at the first annual meeting of the National Society for the Prevention of Cruelty to Children, his last speech.

That month the *Pall Mall Gazette* shocked England by its articles on the white slave traffic in young girls who were traded abroad as prostitutes. Shaftesbury had agitated on the subject for some years without success but Bramwell Booth, the General's son, and the journalist W. T. Stead had actually bought a child as the only way to prove the trade's existence, knowing that they could be put in prison. Shaftesbury immediately tottered round to the Home Secretary and to the new Prime Minister, Salisbury, to support the crusaders and urge legislation.

On 25 July 1885 he left at last for the sea air at Folkestone, which had done him good the previous year, 'where I hope to recover a little strength, and so be permitted to "die in harness."' He was pulled around in a bath-chair, a well recognised figure with his gaunt face and long whiskers. Men doffed their hats as he passed, and children would run up to him. In early autumn he caught a chill, which led to inflammation of a lung; to his distress he became too ill to be moved back to St. Giles's. He wanted to die at home, he said, not 'in a common lodging-house', despite its fine view across the Channel to the cliffs of France.

Each morning he asked for the twenty-third Psalm, and at other times of the day his valet, Goldsmith, or one of the daughters read Bible passages which he chose. Frequently they heard him murmur his favourite prayer, 'Come, Lord Jesus.' All depressions and agitations seemed to fall away. He lay a little restless physically but in peace, mournful that he could relieve misery no more, delighted at the thought of rejoining Minny and Francis, and Maurice, Mary and Conty. The family gathered round. Evelyn had taken Sissy, gravely ill with tuberculosis, to Davos in Switzerland. He hurried back. After some days his father persuaded him that his place was with his wife and he returned to Davos, writing a heart-broken letter of farewell. Other farewells came: Shaftesbury dictated answers to them all.

Colleagues and friends called, but Shaftesbury refused to let the children send for George Holland, now one of his dearest surviving friends, because he might be busy. Vea would let them into the sickroom for a few minutes. He would ask a question or two about mutual concerns, his mind alert to the last. 'I am very ill,' he said to one friend. 'Man can do nothing for me. I am in the hands of God . . . The love of God which is in Christ Jesus our Lord, Yes,' he murmured, 'In His Keeping – with Him alone.' To another he said: 'I know that my Redeemer liveth, and that He has been my Friend for many years.'

Dr. Bowles visited frequently. Accy and Lionel returned when the end was near; Vea, Hilda and Cecil had been in constant attendance. Their father 'conversed with them in the most affectionate and cheerful manner. He expected death, and his gentleness with his children was most touching.'

Millions of homes, great and small, waited daily for the

news from Folkestone. A letter from the Dean of Westminster asked that Shaftesbury should permit burial in the
Abbey. When it was read to him he said firmly, 'No. St.
Giles's – St. Giles's. I want my remains to lie with my wife
and the children in the Family Vault.'

At midday on Thursday 1 October 1885 the sun shone
strongly into the room. When he had listened to the familiar
words, 'The Lord is my Shepherd, I shall not want,' the
children heard him say, 'I am just touching the hem of His
garment,' and they could follow his thought, that soon, like
the sick woman in the Gospels, he would be able to cast
himself at the feet of Jesus and look up, healed, into His
face.

His valet handed him something. 'Thank you,' he said. A
few moments later, at 1.45 p.m., he died.

*   *   *

When the news broke, a great wave of mourning crossed
the land, with a strong desire for a national funeral: some
even wished to override Shaftesbury's wish and insist
that he be buried in Westminster Abbey. A compromise
was reached. His body would be brought to London, to
Grosvenor Square, then carried to the Abbey for a short
memorial service before continuing the journey home.

The funeral of the Duke of Wellington had taken two
months to prepare. For Shaftesbury's, the committee hurriedly set up had only a week to issue tickets and arrange
seating, so that all his interests might be represented. As he
would have wished, 1,000 seats were left unreserved for the
general public. Long before noon on Thursday 8 October,
the time appointed for the service, every seat had been
taken.

All that morning, through a cold heavy rain, ticket
holders were arriving at the Abbey. One hundred and
ninety six missions, schools, societies, hospitals and funds,
every one of which had been his personal concern, sent
representatives. A squad of boys from the *Chichester* and
Arethusa, in sailors' uniforms, marched to their places.

Shoeblacks, girls from the Flower Girls Mission, costers; boys from Industrial Schools; a group of crippled children – twelve deputations in all, of young people and children. They waited quietly in the Abbey, lit only by the daylight and a few candles in the organ loft and the choir stalls.

Outside in the rain the band of the Twickenham Boys' Home was the first to march down Whitehall, with boys carrying a banner: 'Naked and ye clothed me.' Next came the boys from Great Queen Street, scene of the great feast of 1866; their banner had the text: 'I was a stranger and ye took me in.' Group after group arrived, then the sound of the Dead March from *Saul*, played by the costermongers' band, leading a big procession of costers with many banners, who took up position in Parliament Street, which was then a narrow thoroughfare connecting Whitehall, where the pavements were lined with silent mourners, and Parliament Square, which was packed with at least seven thousand people. As the carriages carrying the representatives of the Prince of Wales and other Royalty passed quietly by, their horses with muffled hooves, those inside realised that most of the crowd in the rain were poor people, many in ragged dresses and rough garments but all with at least a piece of crêpe. The slums of London seemed to have converged on the Abbey in a spontaneous mourning such as England had never seen.

All this time the plain hearse, drawn by four horses, and followed by carriages bringing the family and close friends, was moving slowly down the cleared streets from Grosvenor Square. As the procession passed down St. James's Street the clubs drew their blinds in silent respect and every bystander doffed his hat.

In Parliament Street the massed bands formed up as the hearse passed, and marched behind it, playing the Dead March, to Dean's Yard and the door of the Abbey. The coffin, piled high with flowers, was escorted by eight pall-bearers, each having twenty-five years' service with one or other of Shaftesbury's chief concerns.

Met at the Abbey door by the Dean, the Archbishop of Canterbury and many clergy, the procession, led by the choir singing the opening sentences of the Burial Service, moved up the aisle followed by the chief mourners and rank after rank of delegates who had waited in the cloisters. The coffin was placed high in front of the altar, the flowers making a splash of colour in the gloom, with the pall-bearers on either side, the family standing behind.

The Dean began the short service of Psalm, Bible reading, prayers, anthems and a hymn. Looking around at the vast congregation one observer noted that it was not the Lord Mayor or the host of well known names: 'the real significance of the great gathering lay in the indistinguishable but imposing mass of the representatives of humanity . . . the spontaneous homage of whatever is powerful for good in English society.' After the Blessing the service ended with the new organ, while all stood, thundering out Handel's Dead March as a last salute.

The coffin was borne out of the Abbey. The rain had lifted. As the hearse moved towards Westminster Bridge through the silent crowd the costers' band struck up, 'Safe in the Arms of Jesus.'

'When I saw,' wrote Cecil Ashley to his friend Albert Grey, 'the crowd which lined the streets on Thursday as my Father's body was borne to the Abbey – the halt, the blind, the maimed, the poor and the naked standing bare-headed in their rags amidst a pelting rain patiently enduring to show their love and reverence to their departed friend, I thought it the most heart-stirring sight my eyes had ever looked upon; and I could only feel how happy was the man to whom it had been given to be thus useful in his life and thrice blessed in his death, and to be laid at last to his long sleep amidst the sob of a great nation's heart.'

APPENDIX

SHAFTESBURY'S CONCERNS
A CENTURY LATER

Organisations of which he was Founder or President

Shaftesbury Society, formerly the Ragged School Union
Shaftesbury Homes and *Arethusa*, formerly National
  Refuges and Training Ships.
Church Pastoral Aid Society, Mission at Home

British and Foreign Bible Society
Church's Ministry Among the Jews
Dean Close School
John Groom's Association for the Disabled
London City Mission
Missions to Seamen
Open Air Mission
Protestant Alliance
Young Men's Christian Association
Young Women's Christian Association

Organisations of which he was vice-president or patron

Aged Pilgrim's Friend Society
Baptist Missionary Society

Barnardo's
Christian Evidence Society
Church Missionary Society
Curates Augmentation Fund
Intercontinental Church Society
Lord's Day Observance Society
National Anti-Vivisection Society
National Society for the Prevention of Cruelty to Children
North London Homes for the Blind
Railway Mission
Royal Association in Aid of the Deaf and Dumb
Royal Hospital and Home for Incurables
Royal Society for the Prevention of Cruelty to Animals
Seamen's Hospital Society
South American Missionary Society
Spurgeon's Homes
Tower Hamlets Mission
United Kingdom Alliance

INDEX